The Footplate to
THE BOARDROOM
Part 1 - The Footplate Years

RICHARD MACLENNAN

This book published in 2019 by Richard Maclennan
© Richard Maclennan 2019

ISBN 978-1-5272-5033-8

TYPICAL **1982** SCENE AT INSCH. INVERNESS MEN CROSS EACH OTHER WITH LUNCHTIME DEPARTURES FROM EACH END.

ON MY FIRST VISITS TO INVERNESS THIS WOULD HAVE BEEN AN EVERYDAY SCENE. 3 DERBY SULZERS IN THE TANK ROAD.1

Not many people in this industry can claim they have gone from the footplate to the boardroom. However, I am proud to be one of those few. When I took up post in February 2005 as an Executive Director and Board member at Chiltern Railways, my journey from the footplate to the boardroom was realised.

This book is dedicated to the men of the iron road, who down the years have willingly shared their wisdom, humour and tea with a young man who lapped it all up, and will be forever grateful. They helped turn the boy into a man. There are far to many to name individually, but the names of John Hay, Bert Ross, John Nattrass, Dick Forrest and Bob Blackburn will all crop up more than once in this book.

Also, to my fellow Lost Boys of 1968 to 1988: I salute you all, wherever you may be. and at whichever depot you call home.

I hope you enjoy this trip down memory lane as much as I have writing it. This book has been nine years in the making. All photographs are from my own private collection, unless otherwise stated.

Finally thank you to Core 3 printers in Hawick and to my proof readers at the Texthouse in Kelso. Your patience and guidance is very much appreciated.

I am also working on Part 2 of this book, which will cover the management years. This will cover, and hopefully debunk, many of the myths surrounding the perceived benefits of the breakup of British Railways. It will also cover Welsh Freight and all we achieved under the leadership of the late Tom Birch (a man taken before his time), including witnessing the breakup of British Railways and what it felt like on 1 April 1994, when everything changed. Also included: what was it really like at Virgin Trains; how Chiltern Railways, despite its ultra conservative public image, was very much a work hard, play hard company; my time working with the greatest leader of all, Fiona Taylor, former Route Director Sussex; the story of how ScotRail got its HSTs; and the tenacity of one train planner who proved the cynics wrong.

Chapters

WITH SOME OF MY FORMER LOST BOY COLLEAGUES IN 2010

Chapter 1 - How It All Began

My interest in railways was cultivated from a very early age by my grandfather. He had worked on the job during the 1950s, both in Yorkshire and during the summer months on loan at Blackpool. In fact, some of my earliest memories go back to the end of steam in both Yorkshire and Lancashire in 1968, thanks to my long departed and much-missed grandfather.

My grandparents lived near Sowerby Bridge in Yorkshire. As a small child, possibly even pre-school, I recollect standing lineside at various places along the Calder Valley, watching steam locomotives working coal trains between Healey Mills and the Lancashire power stations. The grimy 5F and 8F locomotives were some of the last regular steam workings in the country. The long trains of clanking and squealing grey coal wagons with a brown brake van were a timeless piece of railway history, passing in front of my very eyes. If we were lucky, we would get a friendly wave from the fireman or guard, or even a pop on the whistle in response to my frantic waving. Even more poignant was watching the lines of withdrawn locomotives, minus side rods, being towed by grubby green diesel locomotives to the many scrap yards used to dispose of these rusting hulks. On one trip back from Blackpool in August 1968, the DMU we were on pulled up alongside a grubby Black 5 at the old Manchester Victoria Platform 11, just as the steam locomotive's safety valves lifted with an immense roar. I was never as scared in the whole of my young life, and cried for most of the way back to Hebden Bridge.

Virtually all our family holidays were also undertaken by train. Summer trips to Blackpool, Scarborough, North Wales and Southampton became an almost annual occurrence. Saturday afternoon trips in Leeds and Manchester all helped to cement my love of railways, and the Class 55 Deltic locomotives. Once, my grandfather and I had an invitation from a Kings Cross driver into the cab of **9007 PINZA**, to view events from the sharp end. As departure time approached, I was allowed to press the start button, to fire up the second Napier power unit. My pride soon turned to terror, as the huge engine erupted into life, and once again scared the very life out of me, much to everyone's amusement. With a friendly honk on the horn, **PINZA** eased out of Platform 7 and across the point work, leaving the city in a light blue haze of Deltic exhaust. On a DMU trip back one evening, we emerged from Beacon Hill Tunnel into Halifax station, to be greeted by the sight of **55020 NIMBUS** waiting to head back to Leeds with the empty stock, after arriving with the 1804 from Kings Cross.

My next invitation to the footplate took place on the Keighley and Worth Valley Railway. I had the chance of a short ride on the footplate of **EVENING STAR**, the last steam locomotive ever built by British Railways. As usual, I was scared half to death by this fiery beast. Once the fire-hole door was opened to throw a few rounds on before departure, I had visions of being dragged into the flames and consumed. With such a terrifying introduction to railways, it's a wonder that my interest has lasted this long! Another train, which my best friend forever Shelagh Midgley and I always looked out for, was the Class 40-hauled 5 o'clock parcels train. This service would pass my grandparents' house at around this time, and its whistling 40 and long trains of vans would always catch the eye. Only years later did I learn that this service was none other than *5M48*, the legendary Heaton (Newcastle) to Red Bank (Manchester) empty van train.

Remembering those far-off days takes me right back to those wonderful events. Who can remember the contrasts between the bright, functional Leeds City station and the dark, oppressive atmosphere at Manchester Victoria? The Vic buffet was often frequented by a bag lady, who was old, dirty and very dishevelled, looking for scraps of food, tea dregs and some warmth. To me, she looked like the evil witch from every child's nightmare. In reality, she was probably another victim of a society which appeared not to care. My staunch communist of a grandfather always gave her a few coins and told her to "keep warm, love" whenever we saw her. However, one look from her had me in terror and begging to go outside, or even across to London Road. Some years later, whenever I heard Ralph McTell's evocative song *The Streets of London*, I would think of the buffet at Victoria, and that sad old lady.

Despite its unique charm and interest, the London Midland Region never held the same fascination for me as the Eastern Region. Even trips to London Road to see the clean, silent electrics did not fire my imagination in quite the same way. For me, the best thing about Manchester was a visit to the John Lewis department store in the city centre, to visit the toy department on the top floor. The lift operator had a top hat and smart white gloves – a huge change from the soulless city centres of today. As with many things, this once fine department store has become just another "stack them high and sell them cheap" city centre shop.

Leeds was always my favourite day out, mainly because it involved Deltic locomotives. But we also saw Class 40s and 45s on the North East-South West and TransPennine, as well as the Settle and Carlisle lines. I used to gaze in utter wonder at the window labels of trains such as *The Cornishman, The Thames Clyde Express* and, of course, *The Yorkshire Pullman*. Those window labels always took my young mind to far-off places such as Settle, Carlisle, Dumfries, Edinburgh, London, Exeter and Plymouth. I used to dream that one day, I would visit them all. Thankfully, I finally achieved this ambition, during my many travels between 1978 and 1986. When money allowed, we used to take day trips even further afield, with York, Doncaster, Huddersfield and Chester all being popular. The highlight of arriving at Huddersfield was to run behind the wall to check out the number of the 03 shunting locomotive, stabled for the weekend with its match wagon. These trips were sometimes combined with our other passion of watching Halifax Town FC. The team were doing rather well at the time, in the old third division north, with several good players, such as Bill Atkins. Thanks to some good planning by my grandfather, we nearly always scored, with loco haulage both ways on most trips, too.

On 31 July 1971, Manchester United and their big-name stars, George Best, Denis Law and Bobby Charlton, visited The Shay for a pre-season game in the now defunct Watney Cup. United had been European Champions just three seasons earlier. The match captured the imagination of town fans, and the crowd of 19,965 hasn't been beaten since. The Match of the Day cameras and commentator Barry Davies were also in attendance. The Shay men won the match 2-1, with Bill Atkins nodding the hosts in front on three minutes. They doubled their advantage on 26 minutes, when Bob Wallace converted a penalty, just a minute after keeper Alex Smith saved a spot kick by the away team's Willie Morgan at the other end. Best himself pulled one back for United after converting a penalty he won on 82 minutes. However, Town survived some late United pressure to claim one of the club's most famous ever victories. As Max Boyce would say, "I was there".

Every summer, we used to visit my family in Hythe near Southampton. We always travelled on the 0910 Leeds-Poole train. The trip from Halifax was on one of the ubiquitous Calder Valley units. After this, we always travelled first class to the coast, and mostly had a compartment to ourselves. We often enjoyed afternoon tea of cakes and sandwiches on the run south from Leamington Spa. Traction wise, Holbeck

45s were the order of the day as far as Birmingham, with Class 47s usually forward from there, although the odd Class 33 could work the Reading-Southampton leg, if the larger Type 4 was needed elsewhere. For quite a few years, the reversals at Birmingham and Reading really used to confuse me. I was convinced that the train was heading back to where it had just come from. During the reversal at Reading, I had some of my first encounters with the Western Region hydraulic locomotives. These strange-sounding beasts left quite an impression on me, although they had all been withdrawn by the time my interest in railways really got going.

During our visits to Southampton, I developed a deep love of the sea that remains just as strong today. Long hot summer days spent in Mayflower Park or on Hythe Pier all helped to fire a young boy's imagination for travel and adventure. Southampton was a hugely busy port in those days, and home to both *RMS Queen Mary* and *RMS Queen Elizabeth*. The now demolished Ocean Terminal also played host to the *SS France* and *SS United States* on a regular basis. My grandfather and I stood on the pier with thousands of other well-wishers as the *Queen Mary* set off on her last sailing to retirement in October 1967. She was replaced on Atlantic sailings soon after by the *Queen Elizabeth 2*. To complete another circle of life, I watched the great liner leave Southampton on her last daylight sailing in October 2008, near where I stood watching not long after her delivery from John Brown's in 1968.

In 1972, my family unexpectedly relocated to the Highlands of Scotland, to chase several opportunities brought to the area by the developing North Sea oil boom. For the next few years, my interest in railways all but ceased, other than two trips in 1973: to Thurso with a Class 24 in the summer holidays, and a Class 24 on a Christmas shopping trip on 16 November, with a special Lairg to Aberdeen shopping special.

However, this was all to change in 1974, on my 11th birthday. We left Inverness behind a pair of Type 2 locomotives, and arrived in Edinburgh very late, after some terrible weather conditions en route. Travelling onwards to York, we enjoyed a super run with **55019 ROYAL HIGHLAND FUSILIER**, on a very busy and heavily delayed *Aberdonian*. I have vivid memories of speeding over the Vale of York, enjoying the warm spring sunshine, as Number 19 ate up the miles in the manner for which it was built. This was all very different from the snow and biting wind we had left behind in Scotland. The way home was typically on a Class 47 on the 0845 Leeds-Edinburgh *North Britain* to Edinburgh, before a noisy pair of Class 26 locomotives to Inverness over the Forth Bridge and Ladybank.

In 1977, my parents spent six months working in North Yorkshire, based at Richmond. While my schooling prevented me from joining them, it did allow regular visits to the area and, more importantly, to the East Coast Main Line. On the way down with the removal van, we stopped for a break at Cockburnspath, just as **55017** sped past with a blast on the horn, while working the 1100hrs from London to Edinburgh.

My next visit was during the May half-term holidays. We drove down during the week, after watching Liverpool clinch a record-winning 10th league title, despite West Ham holding them to a 0-0 draw at Anfield. On the Wednesday, I had a flight in a friend's light aircraft. After scaring me half to death with some aerobatics, the flight ended with us overflying my old friend **THE DURHAM LIGHT INFANTRY** on the southbound *Talisman*. If you happened to be on 1E25 that day, and saw a small white aircraft chasing you at low level near Pilmoor, that was probably me.

At the end of the same week, we suffered the disappointment of watching Tommy Docherty's Man United beat Liverpool 2-1 in a very tense FA Cup Final. The disappointment continued when we had the usual Class 47 haulage home on the *North Britain,* on the following Monday morning. However, once back in Scotland, all eyes were firmly glued to the TV to watch Liverpool's first ever win in the European Cup, in the magnificent Olympic Stadium in Rome. What an incredible night and achievement!

On 4 August, we set off for Kings Cross, to spend a week with my family. We had tickets booked for the 1054 from Darlington through to London – a train that I knew could produce a Deltic locomotive, as I had seen one on it numerous times that summer. Sadly, on this day, the operating authorities in Newcastle could find nothing better than a 47 to work the train. The following Thursday, we headed north, and had seats booked on the 1500 from London – a solid Class 47 diagram. We arrived at Kings Cross early, to be greeted by the sight of **55022 ROYAL SCOTS GREY** at the business end of the 1400 to Aberdeen. Despite our best endeavours, we were told our tickets weren't valid on this train, so another 47 trip followed an hour later

This turned out to be my last visit to the East Coast Main Line until May 1978, when my friend Steve and I paid a visit to Edinburgh, on the Bank Holiday Monday. Deltic-wise, it was an excellent day, with **55012 CREPELLO** working the 0745 from London (although by this time an HST diagram), and the 1500 return. **55022 ROYAL SCOTS GREY** worked the down *Flying Scotsman,* with the winged thistle headboard and lone piper awaiting its arrival in Edinburgh. Both these events were to mark the 100th anniversary of the world's most famous train. The day ended nicely, when an immaculate **55016 GORDON HIGHLANDER** arrived on time with the 1055 from Kings Cross. The month of May was an excellent one, as Liverpool won a second European Cup after a 'King' Kenny Dalgleish goal saw the trophy retained at Wembley against FC Bruges.

By the summer of 1978, I was 15 years of age, and had managed to convince my mother that I was now old enough to travel to Yorkshire, and then on to Surrey, visiting relatives with my school friend, Michael. It was 5 July 1978, and at long last the chance for a Deltic trip to Kings Cross: **55006 FIFE & FORFAR YEOMARY** on the *Aberdonian* 1040 Aberdeen-Kings Cross. My luck held out a few days later, when we returned to Scotland with **55015 TULYAR**, all the way on the 0900 from Kings Cross. As we crossed the Royal Border Bridge at Berwick-upon-Tweed, Number 15 had a collision with a very large seagull. On arriving in Edinburgh, the only damage to the locomotive we observed was that the glass in the head code panel had completely shattered.

I was back on the ECML in August, with trips behind **55013 THE BLACK WATCH, 55014 THE DUKE OF WELLINGTON'S REGIMENT** and the ever faithful 'Dirty Little Imps', before heading back to Scotland via *The Clansman* on the WCML. At the time, I was trying to visit every station south of York, to take some photographs of the 55s while they still worked the long distance premier express services. On 15 August, I went to Peterborough and managed to get shots of **55003 MELD** roaring through the station on the down *Aberdonian,* **55008 THE GREEN HOWARDS** on the 1020 ex Newcastle, and **55022 ROYAL SCOTS GREY** on the 1245 to Bradford.

The October half term holiday saw me undertake my first truly solo All Line Rail Rover. The timing of the trip could not have been worse, with no less than 13 locomotives out of service in Doncaster Works. The only locomotives in traffic were **55002/5/6/8/11/12/13/17** and **19**. This was at the height of the power unit problems, and the whole of the ECML was in disarray as a result. I cannot recall seeing a Finsbury Park locomotive hauling a passenger train that week. Somehow, even at such a young and tender age, it really felt as if the locomotives' grip on the premier East Coast passenger services was being loosened. Those glorious summer days of 1977 seemed very far removed from the autumnal gloom.

My final ECML trip took place over the Christmas holidays. However, it was very frustrating to discover that things had not really improved since the autumn. In many respects the ECML had more of a feeling of impending doom than ever. Certainly, the locomotives' impact on the business trains was weakening, and the end of this part of their illustrious careers was imminent.

Back at Kings Cross, on a bitter cold and foggy winter's evening, I was invited into the cab of **55015 TULYAR** as she waited to depart with the 1545 to Leeds. The Kings Cross driver was full of chat and banter. It was a pleasure to spend time in his company, as well as a high note to end the day on, and begin the Christmas Holidays.

The usual family Christmas of overindulgence kept us busy for the next couple of days. The tedium of Boxing Day was broken by Liverpool's 3-0 thumping of Manchester United, in front of nearly 55,000 depressed United fans at Old Trafford. Goals from Ray Kennedy, Jimmy Case and David Fairclough made us smile.

The journey home was spent in quiet reflection, as one does as this time of year. Within six more months, the Deltics' reign on the trains for which they were built was at an end. Life was changing, and to my young mind, not for the better. Of course, as we know now, the Deltic story was not yet at an end. The next chapter for these remarkable locomotives was yet to be written. 1979 was to be a year of change for us all.

On 17 March, I remember my mother telling me that a tunnel had collapsed on the railway near Berwick-upon-Tweed. My first thought was whether a Deltic was inside it at the time. This was not the case, but sadly lives were lost, and the bodies were never recovered, due to the dangerous conditions within the collapsed tunnel.

On 7 April 1979, my friend and I were standing on the concourse by Platform 7, rubbing sleep from our eyes after a rancid WCML *Irish Mail* overnight. We both kept thinking we could see a Deltic with a white roof on the former fuel point. "Deltics don't have white on their roof," said Steve. "It must be a trick of the light." To be frank, I tended to agree with him. Before long, the immaculate white windows of **55003 MELD** made their debut onto the ECML, as she backed down onto the stock of the Kings Cross to the York leg of the *Northumbrian* rail tour. I had a ticket for the tour anyway, and Steve managed to blag himself aboard, so we headed right away to Leeds, with a short leap behind **V2 60800** into the bargain. The white cabs' era was upon us.

Chapter 2 - A Lost Boy at Last

I first heard about the Inverness loco department recruiting further footplate staff while chatting to the signalman at Dingwall, one day in the summer of 1979. He had just put the single line token through the machine, to allow safe passage of the Class 40-hauled air brake Invergordon goods towards Muir of Ord, when the subject came up of what my plans were, now I had left school. "Why not join the railway?" he said, while pulling off the starting signal to allow the whistling giant and its crew to start the final 19 miles of the journey.

Locomotives and coaching stock were to replace the ageing Class 120 DMUs on the Aberdeen road over the winter months, and completely, from March 1980. These units, which first began to work 'over the top' in 1960, had given 20 years of loyal service on the line. They were becoming expensive to maintain due to reliability issues, especially with engines and gearboxes. This DMU service was, to the best of my knowledge, unique. The tablet catcher for the single line was located in the brake van, rather than the driving cab. Therefore, it was the guard's job to check that the correct single line token had been taken on board. He would then advise the driver by bell buzzer communication that all was well, and it was safe to proceed. Fortunately for me, with the replacement Class 27 traction having steam heating equipment, all trains would be double-manned by driver's assistants from Inverness and Aberdeen Ferryhill.

I skipped lunch that day, and instead, used my £1 note to catch the afternoon Class 26-hauled Kyle train into Inverness. I went in search of the requisite application documentation from the admin office above the travel centre. My signalman friend's 'gen' was good, and it was confirmed by the front desk clerical officer that recruitment was about to commence for an additional up to ten posts, with a start date in early 1980.

The application form was returned by post and the waiting game began. About a month later, I was called to interview in the Depot Manager's office at the shed. The interview itself lasted about 30 minutes, with both Tom Haggarty and John Bruce gently guiding me through the process. Both of them used many years of experience to tease the right answers from my bumbling teenage mouth.

I must have said all the right things (with a little help from my friends), as I was soon called for a medical. Then my contract of employment was issued, with a seniority date of 1 February, three days before I actually started work. But who was I to question how BR did its manpower accounting?

On Monday 4 February 1980, I met my fellow traction trainees: George Cook, Derek Wright and Ian Macintosh, onboard the 0815 to Glasgow. We were four strangers brought together to achieve a common objective, although it quickly became obvious that as people, we all had very different aims for the next few months. The journey down from Inverness behind **47207** passed quickly. With my new-found status, I was even more vigilant as to what went on around me, as I looked out for things of interest along the journey, while at the same time showing a modicum of interest in the non-railway chatter of my travelling companions.

We walked through the gates of Haymarket depot just after 1230hrs, to be immediately confronted by the bulk of **THE GREEN HOWARDS** coming on the depot, after working 1S12. This was to be my first official visit to Haymarket, although in the past, I had always found the supervisors amenable to a look round, if they were asked in the right way. We made our way to the training centre. No need to sign in, or undertake site induction briefings, in those days. You were responsible for your own safety, and that of your colleagues. Even as headstrong teenagers, we seemed to manage it without too many close shaves. After settling in, we were introduced to the Senior Instructor, Richard 'Dick' Forrest. Dick was someone I would get to know very well over the next decade. Dick and I used to travel on the 0730 from Glasgow Queen Street together, after I became one of his instructors in 1989. He was a former Motherwell driver, and hugely proud of his west of Scotland roots. He used to revel in working his opinions into the other instructors, most of whom were North British or LNER men, and in terms of railway status and knowledge, far inferior to this bouffant-haired man of the west. He was very much a force of nature: small in stature, but more than capable of holding his own against any opposition. Sadly, like so many of that era, he is no longer with us, and it's now almost 30 years since I last saw him. The other people I remember meeting on that first day were Roy McCarthy and Tam Philphin.

After a quick cuppa in the mess room, we had our introductions to the legendary Tom Skeene. Tam had been a driver at Haymarket, and before that, at Edinburgh's North British shed, St Margaret's. He had, I believe, been removed from driving on medical grounds. Tam had a fierce temper, and many a young trainee had suffered a severe withering for stepping on his recently washed mess room floor, or even worse, asking for an extra biscuit during the morning tea break. He would stand up from his chair or stop what he was doing, and veritably explode when the red mist took hold. The air would be blue for quite some time afterwards. However, I am doing Tom an injustice here; he was a hugely popular and respected man, and would always help you out during times of need. I last saw Tam at the Haymarket Christmas party in 1990. Tam must have passed away now, and is no doubt controlling the biscuit rations in the great mess room in the sky.

Our instructor for the duration of our time at Haymarket was Sandy Wallace, who was already close to retirement, and had left the industry by the time I returned in 1985. In addition to the Inverness contingent, the remainder of our class were made up of two Haymarket and two Eastfield chaps. The Glasgow boys, in particular, came across as hard men from a hard city. However, they soon accepted us 'teuchters', with our strange accents. The forming, storming and norming of the group was soon done and dusted, and all house rules agreed with Sandy. Next, we were issued with our publications, but strangely, not a bag to put them in. The rule in force at that time in Scotland was that only drivers and relief drivers got issued with BR bags. Drivers' assistants had to provide their own. During my five years as a lost boy, I had a motley collection of bags, mainly Gola and Head. Some of my peers preferred the low-cost alternative of a carrier bag turned inside out. It certainly did the job for the non-image-conscious. While working for Virgin many years later, I saw Brian Souter, Chairman of Stagecoach Group, turn up for a meeting in the west wing at Euston with his meeting papers in a carrier bag. Perhaps the bus and rail industries have more in common than we think.

The format of the eight week-long course, or MP11, as it was still known, was as follows:

- Safety (today, this would be Personal Track Safety, PTS).

- Rules and Regulations, as applicable to the grade.

- Train working and signalling.

- Basic traction principles (suck, squeeze, bang and blow, as the saying goes).

- Cab riding (in my case, **55018** around the depot and **47552** to Perth).

- Steam heating equipment (at home depot).

Training ended at 1515hrs every day, to allow those from depots in the west of Scotland, Perth, Dundee, Thornton Junction, Haymarket and Millerhill to travel home. Meanwhile, those of us from further afield spent the week in the Lairg Hotel in Coates Gardens, just at the bottom of the Gorgie Road. I had heard all about the proprietor of the Lairg, but nothing in life could ever prepare you for meeting Alberto for the first time. A huge, hairy bear of an Italian opened the door and said, "watta you foopin want?", before laughing out loud, and telling me I was expected, and to come in. I was told that I was in Room 12, evening meals were at 5pm, and breakfast at 0730hrs and… "no foopin messing me about!"

The Lairg was a comfortable, but basic, affair. Trainees were billeted army-style, with six to a room, and as a result, had next-to-no privacy. There was one bathroom on each floor, and it was very much 'first come, first served'. I have no complaints about how Alberto treated us, and through time, we all came to trust and respect him in our own way.

I very quickly settled into my new routine and really enjoyed my time in Edinburgh. A normal week-day routine would see us in the classroom from 0830-1515hrs, after which most of us would go off and do our own thing. For me, this would mean running to Haymarket Station, if the 1240 from Aberdeen was a Deltic, and riding the train into the Waverley, before blagging a lift in the cab back to Haymarket depot. The first time I tried this, I was given a warm welcome into the cab of **55015 TULYAR**. The next step was to race back to Edinburgh at full speed, to see if a Deltic was working the 1718 to Newcastle, for a ride down to Berwick-upon-Tweed. Even if this was a Class 40, I would still take the train, to put me in position for the 1734 from Newcastle - another train that often produced a 55 and a fair bet for a cab ride back into Scotland. Even then, I was not finished. Next would be a trip to Darlington on 1E35, the 2025 from Edinburgh, for a staff tea in the all-night buffet. Cost: 10p, later going up to 12p in 1981. Finally, I would get the first northbound Deltic-hauled train back to Scotland. This left me less than one hour to get back to the hotel, to wash and shave, and eat breakfast, before the start of another day in class. Quite what my fellow trainees thought of all the comings and goings is anybody's guess. To add some variety to proceedings, I would occasionally overnight to Carlisle instead. This would allow me to watch the endless procession of freightliner trains hauled by pairs of 86 and 87 class locomotives. I would return to Edinburgh on 1S19, the overnight train from Bristol. I never really thought about what would happen if I ever got stuck so far south and missed the start of class. I guess you are more reckless when young. It would have taken some explaining away.

During the course, visits would be arranged by representatives from the drivers' trade union ASLEF, and also the NUR. The railway was a closed shop back then, and union membership was compulsory. The unions must have had some arrangements in place, as ASLEF signed us all up, and the chap from the NUR never arrived.

A further memorable event took place on 4 March. **55007 PINZA** was due to work south on 1E26, the 1945 from Edinburgh to York. This was a train that I had never attempted to cab-ride before. The main reason was it was booked for a Gateshead driver, and also, my favoured train at this time of day was 1E35. On this occasion, for reasons that I cannot remember now, I approached the driver as he waited for departure time, and asked if I could ride to Berwick with him. "Why aye, bonny lad!" was the reply, and I climbed into the cramped cab of the ageing racehorse. I was immediately struck by the fact that we had no working desk instrument lights, and the driver would be 'flying blind', so to speak.

I did not think it appropriate to comment, and thought it best to take the stance of only speaking when spoken to. As we roared out into the night and the darkness of the Lothian countryside, the only light in the cab was the small moon-shaped circle of whiteness from the ETH proving lamp. It's funny how those little things stay in your mind, even after all these years. Once through Prestonpans, the driver began to relax and chat to me about why I was riding about at this time of night. I must admit that most of what he said in his strong Geordie accent, coupled with the whine of Number 7 engines, completely passed me by. After some time, I plucked up the courage to ask him about his lack of illumination and how he could see his speedometer and brake gauges. He laughed and told me we were doing 90mph. To prove it, the cab light was turned on, and I leaned over to observe the needle glued at 90. This was my first experience of old-hand drivers, who could drive by the feel of the road underneath them. Many years of shovelling coal and driving to/from Edinburgh made lighting superfluous for this wise old gentleman. Leaving the cab at Berwick, my thanks was offered for being allowed into the hallowed racehorse cab. A thumbs-up and something Geordie suggested my company had been welcome.

Another incident with **BALLYMOSS** took place on Haymarket depot, towards the end of my training. One morning, our instructor George Burns took us up into the cab of Deltic 18, to walk us through the engine room of this thoroughbred, while running it through the wash road a few times. George Cook and I were the last to go through, when a shout came from the engine room for me to put a key in, as the lights had stopped working. As soon as I put the key into the master controller, one of the big 1650hp engines erupted into life. Shouts and screams emanated from the engine room, and for one horrible minute, I thought I had killed someone. Of course, it was all a huge practical joke which everyone was in on, except me. Even to this day, I am not really sure how they had managed to co-ordinate things so well. I must admit that my heart was still racing, hours later. A cab ride to Inverness aboard **47552** brought down the curtain on an eventful day.

All too soon, the six weeks in Edinburgh came to an end. On the last night in the city, everyone made their plans for how they would enjoy it. In my case, this involved one last week-night trip with a Deltic. In celebration, I took **55005** all the way to York, returning in the early hours of the next day behind **55002** on 1S72, a train which had never once let me down in the whole of those six weeks.

On Monday 17 March, I reported to Inspector Bruce for my MP11 rules and regulations exam. I had met John on the day of my interview, and found him to be a thoroughly decent chap. My view did not change in all the years I was to know him, before his untimely death in 1998. The examination was in the form of questions and scenarios, covering personal safety and the safe working of trains, meaning all fixed and hand signals. Finally, there was the Rule Book section, regarding the protection of trains in an emergency. The entire examination took around three hours. The morning ended with me being given a mild rollicking on the dangers that the railway presented to a headstrong 17-year-old. Some of it must have stuck in my brain, as I used many of those wise words in later life when it was my turn to train and nurture new recruits to the industry. Sadly, I did not heed John's entire message, as I was tragically to find out, six months later. By 1600 hours, I was allowed to go home, as the next morning I had my first shift as driver's assistant. This involved getting up at 3am to be at work by 4am. To celebrate my new status, I joined driver Tommy Day in the cab of **26015** as far as Muir of Ord.

The first couple of shifts involved me doing nothing better than sitting in the bothy spare. Of course, I was never one to sit around doing absolutely nothing, so frequent walks around the shed and over to the station kept my interest levels up. The shed foreman, Adam Sutherland, kindly allowed to me catch the 1110 home on both days, to save me the bus fare. These gestures were always appreciated. The foreman would remember the favour and call it in at a later date, when you would be required to work overtime, or exchange shifts at short notice. It was, I guess, how the railway family looked after each other, and ensured that the train service operated with a happy and contented workforce. In all my years at Inverness, to the best of my knowledge, we never cancelled a passenger train due to shortage of crew.

Wednesday 19 March found me following the now-established routine of the previous couple of days. However, at around 0930, the mess room phone rang, and driver Jimmy Smith and I were requested to attend the foreman's office immediately. Normally, on a 4am start, this could possibly bring the good news that your services were no longer required. The fact that Jim had only booked on at 0800hrs suggested that it was more likely that some work awaited us. Sure enough, our orders were to collect **40175** from the goods yard and go all-speed south. It transpired earlier that day that **26028** and its train of coal wagons had derailed at Dalraddy, between Kincraig and Aviemore, and thus the Highland Mainline was blocked to all traffic. The breakdown train, hauled by another Class 26, was already on site, but a larger and heavier locomotive was needed to re-rail some of the less-damaged vehicles, and remove them from site to Aviemore.

With no oncoming traffic, we made good time and arrived at Aviemore within the hour. We were given the exact mileage of the accident as the 78.5 milepost. Area Maintenance Engineer Bob Taylor, Permanent Way Supervisor 'Big' Bill Gault, and the rest of the breakdown gang, were working hard at assessing the damage, prioritising the work, and planning to reopen the line for the next morning's sleeper and freight traffic. In the meantime, many trains, including the prestigious *Clansman* and *Royal Highlander* services, took the long way round via Aberdeen. If you had seen the damage, you would have wondered if it were possible to reopen within the week, never mind the next 24 hours. **26028** and the first three wagons had remained upright and on the track. The middle six were everywhere: on their sides, ends, and even upside down in someone's garden. The last few wagons were upright but derailed, and had caused some damage to the track as they had come to an abrupt halt, causing great damage to the concrete sleepers.

The plan of recovery was:

- Unload all tools before sending us with the van back to Aviemore.

- Use the steam crane to move a wagon that was in the way of **26028** making any further progress, and to place trackside.

- Recover **26028** and three wagons to Aviemore sidings.

- Send **40175** and tool van back to site to assist with recovery.

- Relief crews for both us and the breakdown train crew to arrive by road by 1500 hours. We would then travel back to Inverness by road transport.

- Removal of all derailed wagons to be completed by 2000 hours.

- Track and signalling cable work to be undertaken overnight, and be completed by 0500 hours, ready for the northbound sleepers to run booked route.

Jim and I finally arrived back in Inverness just after 1600 hours, giving me twelve hours and five minutes on duty. The line reopened the next morning, as planned. Some of the wagons remained at Dalraddy for many months, with one MDA being cut up on site. The upside, if indeed one existed, was that the locals enjoyed free coal for weeks afterwards, as the large debris field was foraged daily. The cause of the accident was established as a broken axle on the fourth vehicle, approximately one mile back down the line. Looking back now, it was a fantastic achievement to get open again so quickly, and is testament to the professionalism and dedication of all those concerned.

On the Thursday morning, I booked on at 0405, after having my twelve hours' rest. A note was found in my pigeon-hole telling me that the following week, I would be training 0800-1600 hours on Stones Vapour, Clayton and Spanner steam heating equipment. The last piece of the jigsaw was about to fall into place. At the time, all passenger trains operating in/out of Inverness had the capability of being operated by a steam heat locomotive. The only exception to this was the up/down *Clansman* service, which was formed of twelve London Midland-region air-conditioned Mark 2E/F coaches. The overnight London sleeper car trains were dual heat stock, and could therefore be operated by either steam or electric heating locomotives.

Boiler training was undertaken by Steve Lewis, one of the senior second men passed to drive. After meeting in the mess room, we shared the first of many cups of railway tea, stewed dark brown from an ancient tea urn that probably had its roots back in the steam era. We made our way down to the wagon shops to have our introductions to the steam heating equipment, in the boiler compartment of **26043**. Steve gave us an interesting overview of how the equipment worked. In simple terms, tubes inside a large copper cylinder had cold water passed through them, across which a burner sprayed atomised air and high-pressure fuel, which ignited and heated the water, turning it into steam. Upon opening a flow valve, the steam passed through the locomotive steam pipe and into the carriages, via interconnecting steam hoses between each vehicle. A high-performing boiler would pass steam through even the longest train, at anything between 40-60psi. Great when everything worked, but misery for the passengers when the equipment failed, as it frequently did. Just before Christmas in 1980, Davie Sutherland and I came home as passengers from Perth, on the internal overnight from Glasgow. To Inverness railwaymen, the train was always referred to as the 0110, its departure time from Perth for many years. By Pitlochry, the heating equipment on the Class 40 had failed, and by Aviemore, ice was forming on the inside of the coach windows. Here we met a Class 26 relief locomotive from Inverness to provide some heat for the remainder of the journey. However, upon arrival in Inverness, I could still write 'ice box' on the inside of the compartment window, so thick was the ice.

By the end of the week, we had operated Stone Vapour/Clayton and Spanner Mark 3 Boilers, or in the case of the Type 2 locomotives, Steam Generators on Class 26, 27, 40 and 47s, plus met the fierce boiler smith, Ernie Kelman. Ernie didn't take kindly to us loco lads breaking his equipment, and causing him to have an even heavier workload than just routine maintenance. On Friday, I was once again up in front of Inspector Bruce for examination. In my case, the exam involved some theory, and operating the Stone Vapour generator in **26045** on the 1110 from Kyle of Lochalsh. I was now a fully-fledged operator, ready to be let loose on the world.

The following week also found me early shift – 0600 spare, to be precise. As the junior man at the depot (I was youngest in age amongst my fellow trainees), I came at the very bottom of the pile when it came to getting a job. Therefore, most of my early days were spent either spare, or on one of the number of depot turns. Monday was spent spare until around mid-morning, when the mess room phone rang and the driver who answered it shocked me into consciousness by asking me to go down to the foreman's office. Jimmy Broadfoot (an ex-St Margaret's driver from Edinburgh) was waiting for me, and told me that **47269** was needed for the 1240 to Edinburgh but required a test run to Culloden Moor and back. This would enable fitters to check out an earlier repair which had hopefully now been rectified. The locomotive and driver (Bert Ross) would be found outside Number 1 road of the main shed, and I should get down there without delay.

Bert, leading fitter Donnie MacLennan (no relation) and I set off for Culloden, running just behind the 1035 London service. After some full-power running up the hill, we arrived at Culloden around seven minutes later. At the time, you could stop outside the Culloden signal box and return to Inverness from the direction in which you had arrived. Bert told me to tell the signalman that as the locomotive had been given a clean bill of health by the travelling fitter and was fully fuelled, we had no need to go back onto the shed, if that made life easier for everyone. By the time I returned to the 47, Bert had changed ends, and to my surprise was sitting in the non-driving seat. "All yours to take back to Inverness, mate", he informed me, with one of his mischievous grins. I told him that I had only been here for two weeks, and had never driven a locomotive before. "First time for everything", he said, "Now, get a move on, as we are in the way of both up and down line traffic sitting here". In essence, I was not really driving anything; all I had to do was release the brakes and coast back down the hill to Inverness, before leaving the locomotive in the goods yard sidings, ready for collection later on by the crew for the Edinburgh. What Bert had done was a masterly stroke in my induction into the footplate grade. He had motivated me in a way that was no risk to him, but highly inspirational for me. Bert and I became great friends, and had many adventures together over the coming years.

The following week I was rostered 1000hrs spare with a rest day Monday. Perfect for me as it meant I could catch the train both ways to/from work. Sadly, other than relieving the crew of **40164** at Rose Street and taking the returning Invergordon goods train into Millburn Yard, the whole week was an endless drudge. It meant sitting in the mess room, reading or learning the numerous footplate card games, such as whist, hunt the jack (or another four-letter word, to those of you in the know) and pontoon.

Thankfully, with the annual leave periods for footplate men now kicking in (back then it would have been possible to be summer leave for the first two weeks in April), my days of sitting around doing nothing were at an end. Tuesday 8 April saw me let loose on the front of a passenger train for the very first time. "Book on at 0515 for turn 02 with driver J Mclean", proudly proclaimed the daily alteration sheet. I can sadly say it was one of the worst days of my young life; my railway bubble was well and truly burst. I waited in the lobby for Jock to book on. He took one look at me and said, "Who the f*ck are you?", before telling the foreman John Robertson that he wanted a second man, not a boy. And with that, he walked away and left me standing there. John said, "Don't worry, it's not you. Away and do your work." I walked dejectedly and alone, carrying the heavy portable radio to look for the locomotives **26034/26044** in the stores road. Not a word was spoken as we ran round to Platform 6. Even then, things didn't get any better. The steam heating pipe on **26044** was bent and it took me five minutes of pushing/twisting and swearing to get the pipes between it and the leading coach connected. All the while, John just stood watching me, feeling, I guess, vindicated about his earlier behaviour. However, in my view, even if he had Charles Atlas as his mate, it would not have been done any quicker. Other than telling me to turn **26039**'s boiler off at Beauly on the return, not a word was spoken between us for the whole day. It was a horrible experience, and I certainly had met someone at the other end of the spectrum from Bert Ross. I am sure Jock must have had his reasons to be such a bitter old man, and he retired a few months later, so this was my one and only shift in his company.

In-cab radios on the north lines were introduced after the severe storms of 1978, when the last train of the day south, driven by Stuart Munro of Wick depot, got heavily stuck in snow drifts 20 feet deep near Altnabreac. With no communication to the outside world, due to the blizzard and high winds bringing down the telegraph wires, the hapless passengers had to spend the night marooned on the moor, until help began to arrive at first light. Such had been the ferocity of the storm, it took four days to recover the locomotives and stock, once all the passengers had been airlifted to safety.

The lessons learned from the subsequent investigation required all locomotives working north of Lairg to carry portable radio equipment, and in winter months, the brake van would carry a hamper of food rations and distress flares. So, from 1979, portable (and very heavy) radios were carried in a bracket in the cab of all Inverness-based Class 26/37 locomotives. The crude, open microphone radio system, using masts in Inverness, Black Isle, Bonar Bridge, Helmsdale and Forsinard, allowed crews and signallers to communicate directly with Inverness control. 'Rail Com North' control could also patch calls through, to allow driver to driver or signaller conversations to take place. To be fair, the system operated successfully until replaced by RETB in 1985.

The next day I went to Aberdeen with **27108** both ways on the 0545 from Inverness, returning with the 0945 from Aberdeen. This was my first encounter with driver JG Munro, another senior man nearing retirement, but a person who was happy to talk, share experiences and offer advice when needed, and drink endless cups of my tea.

John had started his railway career at Forres depot in the 1940s, and therefore had many a story to tell of working double-headed steam over Dava moor with the London sleepers, when booked to run that way before the line's closure in 1965. He had also worked most of the network of former Great North of Scotland lines, which radiated from Elgin to such places as Lossiemouth, Buckie and Banff. None of them survived the Beeching axe, and all had closed by 1968. His own favourite line in the area was the one from Carnie Junction to Portsoy Harbour, possibly for no other reason than sentiment.

The week ended with a couple of shed turns, 0400 Preparation and 0600 Disposal, with drivers Jock Macpherson and Jim Macdonald on the Saturday. Jim was nicknamed 'Snappy', and was another driver who definitely fell into the grumpy old man's club. The 0600 shift was always busy, and we worked like Trojans, fuelling and disposing one engine after another, or shunting the shed to set things up for maintenance, or whatever else our lords and masters had in mind.

My knowledge and experience were growing rapidly, and the following week saw me introduced to the eccentricities of goods traffic and shunting work. Monday 14 April gave me another early book on, this time at 0633. Driver for the day was 'Black Will Macgilvary' (the third member of the grumpy old man's club), and our guard Willie Flood (a real old-time goods guard of the highest order). The job appeared simple enough: take **26014** to Millburn Yard, pick up 18 wagons, shunt Dingwall, Invergordon and Tain, and then swop over at Ardgay with the Wick crew, doing a similar role heading south. All went to plan until we arrived at Ardgay, only to find that our homebound locomotive **26022** had failed with a seized axle, and was incapable of being moved under its own power. Therefore, **26014** shunted the whole train clear of the mainline, to enable passenger trains to operate around us. I was sent to the signal box, to be told on arrival that an engine was coming attached to the mid-morning passenger train, and that we would be here for a good while yet, and not on our way home until around 1330. I returned to the now silent Type 2, to convey the bad news to my colleagues. Surprisingly, both seemed very relaxed about the long wait. After a few minutes, 'Black Will' decided he was off up the street for a walk, and Willie Flood decided to get his head down in the brake van. To my great surprise, Will did not return from his walk until almost 1330hrs. I never knew Ardgay was so big! Whatever he had been doing must have done him some good, as his cheeks had a rosy glow and he was singing about the dancing in Kyle, along with the roads and the miles to Dundee. Perhaps he had walked there, for all I know. As promised, earlier control had done its job well, and **26035** arrived as the pilot locomotive to a sister class member on the 1110 passenger and mail from Inverness. Half an hour later, after some frantic shunting, we were heading for home, with **26022** left behind in the sidings, to be wheel-skated at a later date. After crossing the Class 25-hauled midday smelter goods at Muir of Ord, we had relief waiting for us at Rose Street. We finally booked off duty around 10 hours after starting, and over 11 hours after leaving home, in my case.

Another few weeks of boredom followed, before it was time for my first run over the whole length of the Highland Line proper. Once again, I was 1000 spare, but on both the Monday and the Tuesday I found myself booking on at 1200hrs for the 1240 Edinburgh passenger service, worked by us to Perth, returning on the down *Clansman*, due away from Perth at 1714. The driver on both days was Willie Davidson, better known as the 'Cowboy'. On the first day, we had **40161** to Perth for **47417** back. On the second day, **47120** and **47472** provided the horses. This was my first real experience of top link passenger work. Boiler trouble both days saw me spend much of the trip in the engine room, 'tinkering' to get some heat in the train, as I undertook a steep learning curve in the field of boiler maintenance. After a stroll around the Fair City, a walk down the links, and some fish and chips, we returned to the station just before 1700, in the hope our train would be on time. Inverness drivers didn't seem to like spending much time in the mess room at Perth, for some long-forgotten reason or another. Other than on nights, most drivers would want to go for a walk, "down the street", even on wet or colder days, as opposed to hanging about the fairly basic mess room on Platform 4. Mind you, I did once see a Glasgow driver and a Perth guard square up to each other about which channel the TV should be on. The guard, whose nickname was 'Polyfilla' (allegedly because he was handy for filling things in), won the day. Delia Smith continued her cooking show in blissful ignorance of the near riot, as she enlightened us on how to get our soufflés to come up trumps. On the way back, it was a case of 'hold on tight', as 'Cowboy' lived up to his name, with some fierce driving to win back minutes lost further south. He really was a legend. With the bit between his teeth, and time to make up, he could run an engine like no other, with the exception of his long-time friend, Ian Grant who held just about every record the depot had, other than passenger comfort. I vividly remember one of the few trips I ever had with Ian Grant, or 'The Fugitive', as we all knew him, which involved working **40150** to Perth for another back on 1S07 the *Royal Highlander*. Control tried to keep 40s away from this job, as so much time could be lost with a loco in poor health. Ian was having none of it, and he hammered his locomotive without mercy, as no train he ever drove would be late if he could help it. At one point, I questioned him about why the yellow lineside speed board said 65mph when he was going a little bit faster (or "running cheery", as he called it). "Listen loon (boy)", he said. "Yon boards are for inexperienced drivers, and only a guide for men of high experience such as myself." I thought it best not to question his logic about when, in his eyes, inexperience would turn into experience. Coming off the Slochd, it felt like the downhill slalom at the recently held winter Olympics.

The summer of 1980 was the beginning of the end for many footplate and workshop staff at Inverness. The 1970s oil boom had reached its peak, and already traffic was slowly being lost to road, or its source closing down or being mothballed. The UK economy was slipping into recession, and the shadow of Thatcher and her nasty thugs was on the horizon. Even the traffic which remained would often be cancelled, or run engine and brake van, to balance the motive power for subsequent workings. One source of traffic, which, for now at least, continued to buck the trend, was the British Aluminium smelter at Invergordon. We had a morning and an afternoon shift serving this location. The morning job left Millburn Yard at 0653, conveying traffic which had arrived overnight from Sighthill and Mossend. The requirement for an air brake-fitted locomotive would see, more often than not, a Class 25 or 40 provided for the job, depending on the load to be conveyed on the return trip. One day during early summer, Davie Sutherland and I had a good trip with a Class 40 on this run. After a huge shunt in the smelter itself, with wagons flying hither and thither as they got bumped by the 133-ton locomotive and its increasingly irate driver, we were almost ready to go. Traffic was particularly heavy, and so big was the train, we had to bring it out of the smelter in two portions. The first portion was aluminium ingots conveyed in OBA wagons, and the second was alumina dust conveyed in covered hoppers. After much heavy shunting in Invergordon, we finally had the whole train lashed together and ready for home.

It was quite simply the longest train I had ever seen this far north, and almost filled the passing loop from end to end. The guard came up and gave Davie the load sheet and driver's slip. I cannot remember how many wagons we had, but like Davie, I was surprised when it appeared we only had just over 900 tons on the back. Davie was a frequent user of Anglo-Saxon language, and not a great lover of goods guards, but equally, time was ticking. As his home was in Aviemore, he also usually had one eye on the clock, with an infrequent passenger service home at the time. He could just not believe that this monster train of fully loaded vehicles, was under the maximum load of 1,000 tons for this class of locomotive and route. As a novice, I tended to agree with him, as we struggled to get the train on the move and out onto the single line beside the Moray Firth.

We managed to make Dingwall without much fuss, but after waiting for the late-running midday Wick train, the hardest task was still ahead: the 1:100 all-out assault of Conon bank. We had just about got up to 40mph as we passed the stone viaduct over the river. However, speed quickly dropped off on the climb, with us soon down to walking pace as the whole train got onto the gradient. The amps were almost off the clock, such was the unequal struggle faced by this veteran locomotive. Without fear of exaggeration, I could have got out and walked ahead of the train the last few hundred yards to the summit, by Conon Mains farm. Thankfully, with no other traffic about, we had a clear run for the remainder of the way into Inverness. By the time we propelled the train back into the yard, it was not only the locomotive which was hot and bothered - so was Davie. He immediately went into the yard supervisor's office and demanded someone count the load of his train. This was done, and the true load we had hauled that day was 1,215 tons. Suffice to say, the guard had by this time slunk away. However, with no real harm done, and another lesson in life learned, we dropped the 40 onto the shed and went our respective ways, as Davie berated the guard's parentage, to anyone who would listen.

The summer timetable always brought extra work for junior men at any depot, and Inverness was no exception. Within the next few weeks, I enjoyed trips to Kyle of Lochalsh, Aberdeen and Perth with **26045**, **27003** and **37144** respectively. I still did not have a regular driver, but seemed by chance to spend a fair amount of time with Ted Manson and Louie Shaw, characters at differing ends of the personality spectrum. Ted was slightly aloof, and at first appeared cold, until you got to know him, whereas Louie was an open book, and always made you feel welcome in his company. Ted's values were very much still in the steam era, and I soon learned he appreciated the little things, such as the cab being swept for him, or the windows cleaned. If you did such things of your own free will, the barriers soon came down, and the personality of an excellent engineman appeared.

One of the main problems I was still encountering was not being able to drive, living some 20 miles from the depot. Relying on public transport and lifts was clearly going to be unsustainable. It was my mother who first suggested I needed to think about taking lodgings. Nothing more was said for a few weeks, until copies of the Inverness Courier were left around the house, with various potential lodging houses highlighted in red pen. In August I moved into a ground floor studio flat in Crown Circus, and for the first time, the ability to walk to work was mine. Of course, things never go as smoothly as planned, and within my first week of living alone, I managed to sleep in for work twice. How ironic, after months of long-distance commuting without incident, that I should find myself in this position. On the second occasion, I arrived 40 minutes late for the 0400 preparation turn, only to be told by the foreman Jimmy Broadfoot that as I must be tired, my services were not needed that day, and I should go home and get some more sleep. Jimmy's most used expression, when he was displeased with you was, "you're not on, cock". In this instance, this meant the loss of a whole day's pay, on a week that contained little overtime or enhancements. I was certainly going to notice it in my pay packet the following Thursday. The medicine must have worked, as I was never late again for several years. It was man management at its best. The first occasion, I was given the benefit of the doubt, and on the second occasion I was punished, without the need for anything more formal than a stroke of Jimmy's red pen. It never even entered by head to complain to anyone about the situation. I had let the side down, and was punished accordingly.

During the summer months, I had my first experience of the bridge inspection train. This train would tour the country, checking the under-arch condition of bridges and viaducts. I managed to pick it up off 2000 spare on Wednesday. We set off, with the small train hauled by **26039**, and after going to Dingwall, to allow the engine to run round the train, and to fill our mash can, we positioned ourselves on Conon viaduct, ready for a night of what can only be described as brain death. The team working the inspection boom must have checked every single brick of the viaduct at least twice, and even my driver, Dan Wares, commented that he hoped they worked at a faster pace when they built the viaduct in 1860. So long was the job, we had crew relief at 0300, as the inspection was due to continue until the line opened for traffic at 0600. To be fair, the guys were only doing their jobs. Thankfully, this was to be my only trip inspecting bridges for some time.

As the summer months turned to autumn, the sight and sound of Class 40s on Highland passenger trains became less frequent. More and more trains were becoming 47-hauled, with locomotives from depots far and wide, especially Cardiff Canton and Crewe, for some strange reason, putting in appearances in the town. While the additional power of the new machines was welcomed by crews from both Inverness and Perth, one downside was the propensity for 47s to catch fire, following sustained periods of heavy braking. For a while, it became an almost weekly event for one of these machines to arrive in Inverness ablaze, after the long descent from Slochd. I personally witnessed both **47211** and **47520** suffer severe under-frame conflagrations, as a result of this phenomenon.

Various solutions were tried to rectify the situation, including more frequent under-frame cleaning, changes to the brake timings, increasing the brake pressures on the coaching stock to reduce the amount of braking undertaken by the locomotive, and also instructions to crews to brake lighter and earlier. All these mitigations helped, but it was only the near destruction of an ETH machine through fire that a more technical solution was found. This solution was the mandatory fitment of non-phosphorous brake blocks or, as we called them, non-spark blocks, for any Scottish-based locomotive which regularly worked up the middle, over the big hills to Inverness. Almost overnight, the situation was resolved, and the sight of trains dropping down into Inverness with twelve Catherine Wheels under the locomotive became a thing of the past. The last brake-induced fire that I can remember was on the 47-hauled 1310 from Glasgow, when Davie Irvine and I had to rescue the stricken train up in the pass of Killiecrankie with our two Class 20 locomotives, which had been removed from the empty cement train we were working to Perth. With the errant and still smouldering brush left in the engineers' siding at Blair Atholl, we reattached the 20s for the Perth crew to take forwards to Inverness, while we travelled home on the cushions to Inverness. This was perfect for Davie, as he lived in Aviemore and got home three hours sooner than planned.

With the first tinges of autumn in the air came a return to the spare link. The peak summer holidays and additional traffic was now abating, so card schools and reading would once again be the order of the day. Thankfully, I was returning to the wilderness of spare working as one of the senior spare men, and therefore would be first in the pecking order for any mainline work which came our way. Since May, a number of additional drivers' assistants had been recruited, including John and Angus Blackstock (both grand boys on the pipes and members of the Inverness pipe band), Jimmy Johnson, who would become a good friend for a number of years, and last but not least, Mick Tough and Kevin Mackintosh, both of whom are still colleagues at our current employer. Although summer passenger loadings had declined, freight work showed a welcome increase, with both household coal and rock salt being moved north in bulk, ready for the long winter months. One evening, when booking on for 2200 spare, the foreman, Jock MacAngus, told me that I was to travel passenger with driver Willie Macdonald and guard Willie Flood, on the 2350 passenger train as far as Dalwhinnie, to collect a train of coal which had been left in the siding by a Perth crew. Arriving in Dalwhinnie, we found our train in the location described and set about making **27030** ready for the task ahead. Our timing was perfect, as no sooner were we ready to depart, than the Class 25-hauled Sighthill to Inverness Class 6 freight shot through the station and onto the single line section ahead. Our spluttering 27 pushed the short, but heavy, little train out onto the mainline, to await our own clearance to proceed north. The 25 must have been making good time, as we soon had section clearance and were on our way.

Willie soon had the train bowling along at its maximum speed of 45mph, and with the train ahead having a higher maximum of 60mph, we both swept north on a string of green signals. All was well, until dropping down from Daviot to Culloden, we sighted Culloden distant signal at caution, and as we came off the viaduct, the home signal was at danger. Our initial thought was that some problem lay ahead of us. However, as we approached the red, it slowly cleared, which was a sign that the signalman wanted us to stop at the box, to enable them to convey some message or other. Sure enough, a red light from the box confirmed our suspicion. Apparently, the crew of the Class 25 had stopped to report that they had been followed by an unidentified flying object, all the way from just below Moy, to Culloden viaduct. The object, whatever it was, flew beside the locomotive, about 50 feet away, between the railway and the hill tops to the east. As the train passed over Culloden viaduct, the object turned away to the right and flew down the valley towards Nairn, before shooting skywards and out of sight, in the blink of an eye. Whatever it was, we confirmed that we had seen nothing out of the ordinary, nor had we observed any damage to the railway. I have no doubt the crew involved, driver Bert Ross and his assistant Dougie Fox, must have seen something which made them stop the train, to report the matter to the signalman and later, control. Several months later, on the same train, at the same location, with the same traction type, this time **25235**, with me in the driving seat, Bert talked me through exactly what had been seen, and it was obvious he was speaking with sincerity. Another one for the railway X Files, I guess.

On the Friday of the same week, I was required to book on at 2010 to work the up *Royal Highlander* to Perth, returning into Inverness at 0440 with the internal overnight. The driver on the turn was Jimmy MacDonald, or 'Helmsdale Jim', as we knew him. We had a non-descript run to Perth, and on the return, had Haymarket's **47040** as motive power. Jimmy kindly let me drive his engine out of Perth, and as we headed out into the open countryside, we could tell that a wild, stormy night lay ahead. We slipped all the way up Kingswood bank, and both of us commented that if Drumochter was this bad, we would struggle without assistance. The Dunkeld distant signal was at caution, as the home was being held at danger. Once again, a signalman wished to pass a message to us, and as we rounded the corner towards the box, following the clearing of the home signal, a red hand signal came into sight. With 15 vacuum-braked coaches to control, I needed to make careful use of the brake, and somehow managed to get the train to glide to a halt, with my window next to the box window. Talk about stopping on a sixpence – the signalman was most impressed. "That was an excellent stop, son", he proclaimed. Coming from a former steam fireman, this was praise indeed.

The message to be passed was that the train ahead of us, the Winsford rock-salt train, had reported low-hanging branches on the exit from Inver tunnel, and we were to proceed at caution at this location. We crawled out into the darkness of the night, never exceeding 40mph, just in case the mileage had been incorrectly reported, or in case some other unseen hazard lay ahead of us. Inver tunnel was one of those tunnels which almost looked too small for trains to actually fit through. The road, the railway and the river Garry all had to fit through the narrow pass at this location. As we entered the tunnel, speed was further reduced to 20mph, as two pairs of mark one eyeballs peered into the void. What must be remembered is that this all took place before locomotives were fitted with headlights, and the only illumination available was from the extremely dim marker lights, and often a bardic hand lamp, shining out of an open window. About 150 yards north of the tunnel, we caught sight of the offending tree. Most of the branches had been mangled by the previous train, but a couple still proved to be a potential hazard to windows, or anyone daft enough to have their head out of the window. We stopped the locomotive, and alighted from the footplate to make good the offending objectives as best we could, with a little help from Jim's trusty penknife, in a 'boy's own' clearing-up job. Permanent way staff would no doubt clear up all the debris during the course of the day. With the drama safely and sensibly dealt with, the big 47 was opened up, and we rasped along the valley, past the wonderfully named Inchmagrannachan level crossing, and on to Pitlochry, which tonight, due to our lateness, would be our crossing point with the up overnight.

At Aviemore, the station dwell time was always at least 10 minutes or more, as mail and newspapers were unloaded for much of Spey valley, as had no doubt been done for the last 100 years. While all this activity was taking place, I would fill up the boiler water tank from the high-pressure hose, which at the time was located by the down starting signal. The reason for this act of altruism: the last job of our night shed men was to fuel and water this locomotive, and by filling the tank now, it would help them complete their task that little bit quicker, and get home to bed. The shed turns at the depot were some of the longest and hardest we had – the few turns where a degree of manual work still took place. On the night turn, which was 2200-0600, you would be flat out for most of the time. After booking on, you would take the locomotive for the up overnight to the station, couple on and pre-heat the train. You would then fuel and dispose of the engines from last trains arriving north, south and east. The next job was to prepare the locomotive for the 0110 NPCCS to Perth. After catching your breath, the night's shed shunting would then begin. Depending on maintenance requirements, this could be heavy going. Shunting dead locomotives would involve the use of a link coupling and a shunting pole. The coupling itself weighed about half a hundred weight and may have to be carried around the shed several times. Using the shunting pole took skill and dexterity, and many an unwary person had come unstuck when things went wrong. After setting up the shed for fitting staff, which would often take until around 2am, you could then adjourn to the mess room for refreshment. After brief respite, the next task was to dispose of locomotives arriving on shed from incoming freight trains. Depending on traffic requirements, this could be anything up to six to eight locomotives, if all trains had run and also produced booked traction, which for two of them, involved pairs of Class 20s. These particular trains were the Oxwellmains to Inverness cement train, and the Ardrossan to Culloden Moor tanks. We also had a train of gas tanks which ran to Invergordon, but as the 20s would usually work through, this train recessed in Millburn Yard, and the locomotives did not come onto shed until mid-morning. Next, it was time to prepare the Class 08 for the driver booking on at 0345 station shunt, or passenger yard, as it was known. This locomotive only came on shed every other night for fuel and servicing. The rest of the time, it was stabled in the carriage sidings.

For me and my colleagues, the hardest part of the night was always the wait for the overnight locomotive to come onto shed. This was usually around 0500. This would leave the fuel road clear for the day shift. Also, as the internal overnight loco was next rostered to work the 0815 to Glasgow, it would be all gassed up, ready for the 0400 prep lads. Therefore, you would only have a few minutes left to wash up, before leaving the premises just before 6am.

THE AUTHORS CAR ALONG WITH **47472** CLIMBING OUT OF TOWN WITH A PRE CHRISTMAS CLANSMAN.

THE RMS QUEEN MARY LEAVES HER HOME PORT OF SOUTHAMPTON FOR THE FINAL TIME IN 1968

THE MANCHESTER VICTORIA OF MY CHILDHOOD-COPYRIGHT RAIL-ONLINE.CO.UK

FILEY, 1960'S. ONE OF OUR SUMMER HOLIDAY DESTINATIONS.

LAST DAYS OF STEAM. SUCH A MACHINE TERRIFIED A 4 YEAR OLD AUTHOR.

DRIVER LOUIE SHAW OPENS UP **37114** AFTER A SUCCESSFUL TOKEN EXCHANGE AT LENTRAN IN JUNE **1984.**

JOCK 'ALLANFEARN' MACKENZIE WAITS PATIENTLY WITH HIS **08** PRIOR TO SHUNTING THE FIRST WICK ARRIVAL IN **1983.**

Back at Aviemore now, with a full tank of water, Jimmy took control for the last leg into Inverness. This involved humping the heavy train over the Slochd, before a high-speed dash downgrade into Inverness. The train at the time was booked to bypass the station and reverse into Platform 6 – no mean feat, with a dozen or more vehicles on the back. Back-to-back radios and just a lamp from the rear of the train, a few feet before kissing the platform buffers. After stopping, the engine was tied off and straight onto the shed. This allowed the station pilot to detach the leading four vans to go onto the front of the stock, for the 0615 to Wick in Platform 5, and one van to go onto the stock of the 0655 to Kyle of Lochalsh in Platform 7. The remainder of the train would eventually be shunted into the carriage sidings, after all the sleeping car passengers had alighted, no later than 0730. Slick efficient railway operating at its very best.

The 0615 to Wick was the most important train on the far north. It would often load to nine vehicles – a considerable load for a small locomotive at any time of year, but even more so in autumn and winter. I remember one morning in November 1980, when **26015** slipped to a stand on Lairg bank, despite the best efforts of driver Louie Shaw to overcome this considerable incline. When working this train at this time of year, the last thing you wanted to see was a passenger waiting to join at Invershin. This would result in a standing start up the 1 in 70 gradient to Lairg. The load on this particular morning was the full 315 tons, with vans full of mail in the lead-up to Christmas. We had suffered station overtime at Invergordon and Ardgay, and **26015** was being worked hard to win back the minutes. Coming off the shin viaduct, the power was being wound on for the climb, when the sight we dreaded came into view. A lady was standing with her arm out to signify she wanted us to stop. Louie was a gentleman, so if he did curse, it was under his breath. With a great show of dexterity, the power handle was closed, and the brake applied, in one quick easy move. Station duties complete, and off again, except we slithered more than started. We slipped and slid round the curve, but as the whole of the train came onto the bend, its weight, along with the drag factor, brought us to a shuddering halt. Try as we might, the train would not move for any significant distance without slipping. Different settings of power controller were employed, to no avail. All that remained was for me to walk ahead of the train, to drop sand on the rails to aid forward momentum. At the time, during October and November, we always carried a couple of carrier bags full of dry sand on the footplate for such an eventuality. My arms ached from carrying the bags, but the golden sand did its job, and slowly but steadily, progress was made, and momentum gained. When my bags were empty, I stood back and admired my handiwork, as Louie shouted out of the window for me to wait there and he would pick me up on the way back. To be honest, I had no choice. Where else could I go in the middle of nowhere, on a damp November morning? Thankfully, Louie was good to his word, and appeared 15 minutes later with **26032**, on the first up train of the day.

As November turned into December, my life was about to change forever. Booking on duty at 0615 on Friday 5 December would be the last time I presented myself at the timekeeper's window for nearly six months. My booked work that day was with driver JG Munro, on the pick-up goods to Lairg. We collected our locomotive **26035** from the stores road, and made our way to Millburn Yard. Our short train of coal and vans had already been made ready by the guard, and the swirl of smoke from the brake van suggested he had a good fire going for the morning's work. This was to have been my last turn of duty ahead of a week's holiday, which I had planned to spend travelling on the ECML, and be in position for the release from Doncaster Works of **55002** in green livery. For my plan to work, I needed us to be back in Inverness by 1400, to enable me to change and travel on the 1448 to Edinburgh, to meet up with friends that evening.

Maybe I was rushing, or preoccupied, but something made me oblivious to the still-moving **26035**, as I walked into its path, catching one of the large shiny buffers in my chest, and being knocked into the leading coal wagon of our train. With a buffer in my chest, and another in my back, I knew for certain that I was about to die. Indeed, I can confirm that your life, however short, does flash before your eyes at this time. If it had not been for the timely intervention of the guard, Brian Leech, my life would have ended at 0647 that day. He had decided to take a final walk around the train, checking hand brakes, when he came across me in my death throes. My next memory is waking up in hospital, having my uniform cut off my body, which was smashed to pieces. I had broken every rib, had a collapsed lung, fractured collarbone and had twisted my spine, to such an extent that I will have back pain for the rest of my life. By the time I finally left hospital, I was bruised from my neck to my knees. I was bed-bound for six weeks, and suffered pain that can only be described as excruciating. Everybody from the railway was spot on, and I have no complaints whatsoever about the chain of care I received afterwards. I blamed nobody but myself, as I continue to do even today. Gaining compensation for my injuries did not enter my head, and maybe it's why today, I struggle with the ambulance-chasing victim culture in society. My only regret is the suffering I must have caused the late John Munro, who was never the same again.

As I lay in bed, dosed up on morphine, one of the greatest musicians of our age, and an advocate for peace, John Lennon, was shot dead in New York on 8 December. The ex-Beatle was only 40 years of age, and had so much more to give this world, had he lived. I never have to think, even for a second, when asked if I can remember where I was the day Lennon died.

After missing almost six months of work, and a phased return to work under the wing of ASLEF rep. Peter Mackenzie, by June 1981, my life was beginning to return to normal. Once again, I began to work the full range of shifts at the depot. In the time I had been away from the workplace, many familiar faces had retired, and another eight driver's assistants had started work. Men who had started life on the railway during the years between the Great War and World War Two were now reaching their 65th birthday, and as they left, men in their 50s, such as Frankie Boyd and Duncan Finlayson, were at last being promoted to the grade of driver, after 20 years or more as relief drivers or passed men. It seems incredible now, but back then, at certain depots in Scotland (Aberdeen Ferryhill being one), men could retire at age 65 without ever being a booked driver.

Significantly, by the summer of 1981, most HML passenger trains were now in the hands of Class 47 diesels. The sight of Class 40 or 26 hauled trains was almost a thing of the past. 40s, if they did put in an appearance, did so either on freight trains, or having come over the top from Aberdeen. So much was changing, as the fledgling business sectors began to strip out perceived inefficiency from the network. Already, places such as the Kyle road were seeing little or no freight traffic. Summer passenger loadings were much lighter than in previous years, and a general air of utter despondency hung over the depot. I suspect we always look back with rose-tinted spectacles. However, I am certain that 1980 was the last year of the old railway, and by 1981, the bells of significant change tolled across the whole of the BR network. Much of my work that summer was either on the Aberdeen or north roads, I did enjoy a couple of trips to Perth, the most notable of which involved **26021** and a classmate on the 1240 to Edinburgh. The driver was Joe Polson, another chap who had transferred into Inverness when Keith depot closed in the 1960s.

During this period, I had my furthest trip north ever with a Class 40. We had one such machine on the Invergordon goods one morning. I cannot be certain, but I believe it to have been **40181**. The driver's name escapes me, too, but the guard was once again Donnie Leech. I had been with this driver all week, in what was his final week before retirement. He had allowed me to do all the driving, as he was obviously in exit mode, and looking forward to the life ahead. We had a couple of additional OBA wagons, which were needed at Fearn, to be loaded with potatoes. We left Inverness, running hard behind the 0655 to Kyle, and made good time to Invergordon. The trick then, with this particular job, was to be ready to depart for the smelter, as soon as the Tain signalman had given train out of section for the first down passenger train. It would then be a case of all speed to smelter, and lock the train in the complex by use of the ground frame.

This haste was down to the fact that always had the whereabouts of the 1115 Inverness to Wick service in mind. On a busy day, you would want to complete all of your shunting, to get back out of the smelter and into Invergordon for its passing, especially if you needed to shunt MK Shands or the Invergordon distillery as well. On a quieter day, it would be possible to get back to Dingwall to meet the passenger service there. This day was going to be the former, and not the latter. Shunting at this location was always complex. It was a case of getting the train onto the reception road, and then placing the entire individual wagons where needed. The OBAs would go right round the back of the smelter for loading with aluminium ingots, for onwards transit to various parts of the UK. The hoppers would be placed under the bunker for loading with alumina dust, for which the main customer was the Lochaber smelter in Fort William, less than 100 miles by road, but over 300 by rail. Finally, fuel tanks were placed at the discharge point for unloading. To enable all this to take place efficiently, the calibre of the guard would come to the fore. With a good guard, it would be easy and almost a work of art.

The finest man I have ever seen shunt the smelter was the late William Flood. By this time, Willie was in his 60s, but he worked like a Trojan, and would get the job done in half the time of a younger man. Even in the height of summer, he would strip down to his shirt and tie (he was old school, and even as a goods guard, always wore a collar and tie), and graft like no other. The sweat would be running off his body by the time he was finished. Even the most callous driver's assistant would find it hard not to get down onto the ground to help. His speciality was 'fly shunting'. This involved getting a whole rake of wagons on the move with the locomotive, before Willie would use his shunting pole to uncouple us as the train was moving. We would then charge round the corner with the locomotive, as Willie expertly pulled points, uncoupled wagons, and sent them scurrying in all different directions.

If the speed of the wagon was too great, it would crash into the buffer stops, and possibly derail, and if it were too slow, it would not clear the hand points, and block the locomotive in a dead-end siding. This was a disaster, as now everything would come to a grinding halt. Worst case scenario would then require another locomotive to come from Inverness to rescue the situation, which meant a huge delay, lots of report writing and possible disciplinary charges for all involved. This situation only ever happened to me once, and that was with the same guard who had miscalculated the weight of the train with Davie Sutherland. In fact, it may have even been on the same week.

On this day we had a Class 25, and all had gone to plan, until the last three wagons did not have sufficient speed to reach their intended destination. With over half of the rear OBA blocking our exit, we were well and truly marooned. Red faces, along with the prospect of a huge delay. In an effort to redeem himself, the guard arranged with smelter staff to borrow a tractor and a length of steel rope. He reckoned that by making a noose with the rope and hooking it round the buffer of the leading OBA, he could tow it sufficiently clear to facilitate our escape. The driver claimed he was having nothing to do with things, and told me to stay on the engine, well out of the way. The steel cable, which was at least half an inch thick, was attached as planned, and the tractor engine gunned to facilitate movement. Immediately, the strain on the wire was apparent, and before the wagons even moved, the steel wire snapped with a pistol sound, and the steel smashed back into the wooden body of the OBA, causing a deep gash across several of the planks. I understood why I had been told to stay in cab, as if the wire had hit anyone, it would have chopped them in half, like a cheese-wire through red Leicester. Salvation finally came in the form of a friendly JCB driver, who used the front bucket of his yellow 3C machine to nudge the wagons down grade, and sufficiently clear to allow us to inch past with our 25.

Back to **40181** and with all the smelter shunted, all that remained was to propel our Fearn wagons out onto the mainline, run empty to Tain to run round them, and then back to Fearn for the guard to open the ground frame. That would enable us to set back into the trailing siding, couple off the wagons and then light engine back to Invergordon to collect our loaded wagons for Inverness. To this day, sitting aboard the 40 at the north end of Tail loop remains the furthest north I have ever been on one of these fine EE machines. I am unaware if one ever went further north in the BR era, but it's not beyond the realms of possibility that a class member may have reached Lairg or Brora at some point in their association with the Highlands.

Some further notable events from the summer of 1981 involved trips to Aberdeen and encounters with Deltic locomotives. On the first occasion, Dan Wares and I had taken **27021** over on the second train of the day. The diagram showed us being relieved by a set of Aberdeen crew, before taking our meal break and relieving another Aberdeen crew, and heading back to Inverness with the 1150 service. Not long before departure, and much to my delight, I heard the droning which heralded the arrival of **55010** into Platform 5 with the 0855 from Edinburgh. My delight turned to euphoria when I saw my old friend Gary Ormiston in the driving seat of Number 10. A few hasty words were exchanged before I had to leg it up Platform 6 to join Dan and another Class 27 for our trip home. A few weeks later, Jock Hay and I took **27005** to Aberdeen on the 1240 service. This diagram required us to go to Ferryhill depot to bring a fresh locomotive up to the station to re-engine the 1750 to Inverness. After a routine trip over from Inverness, we left the 27 with the Aberdeen men, and went to look for a lift to Ferryhill depot. It just so happened that 1S12 had been Deltic-hauled into Aberdeen with the locomotive requiring fuel upon arrival. With perfect timing, Jock and I climbed into the cab of **55021** for the short trip to Ferryhill – a most unexpected bonus.

Whenever I look back on 1980 and 1981, it saddens to me realise how much of the railway at this time was in terminal decline. At the time, I was too young and near the action to see that the battle for the very future of the industry was underway, and in many parts of the country, the battle was being lost. During the summer, Aberdeen was re-signalled, and the three mechanical boxes we dealt with, along with a plethora of semaphore gantries, were all swept away, to be replaced by colour lights and a modern power box. Even in the Highlands, things were declining rapidly. Daily freight traffic to Wick ceased in a few more months, and Howard Doris traffic at Stromeferry had ceased to run, rendering the private siding and shunt locomotive surplus to requirements. Rusty rails at numerous sidings and goods yards throughout our region showed just how infrequently they were being used. It was only when we lost the second of our Invergordon freight jobs, or the 12 noon goods as it was known, did it hit home how serious things were becoming. With the end of the summer timetable, a whole bunch of drivers and driver's assistants were deemed surplus to requirements, me included, and the dreaded spare link re-created for the winter months.

For the period from October 1981 to May 1982, I was paired with up with driver Jimmy MacDonald, 'Helmsdale Jim'. He was definitely one of life's characters, and one could not wish for a better driver to spend time with. An example of his kindness came one wet evening in November. We had been given **26011** to work a special freight to Perth, before coming home passenger on the internal overnight. All was well as we set off from Millburn Yard and out under the A9 to begin the climb to Culloden Moor. About halfway up the climb, with the speed just beginning to balance at around 20mph, we heard a bang, followed by a loss of power, and then the engine stopped. Jim went into the engine compartment to investigate matters, and reported back that the heat exchanger had failed, and all of our cooling water had been lost. This particular piece of equipment was situated on the floor on B bank of the power unit. Its primary function was to cool the lubricating oil by transferring the heat from the oil to the cooling water. This kept the oil at the correct temperature and viscosity, and allowed the heat to be dissipated, as the water passed through the radiators. The water jacket within the heat exchanger had obviously failed, thus allowing all the water to escape. Jim told me that I now had one of two choices: walk and request assistance (the nearest phone was two miles ahead of us), or go into the engine room and hold the engine governor over-ride lever for the remaining four miles to Culloden. Neither option filled me with joy. However, with the former I would get wet, and with the latter, hot and sweaty. I elected for the engine room, and for the next ten minutes I had to wedge my body between the crankcase and the engine room wall, and hold the seven-inch silver lever for all my worth. This was no mean feat, for as much as I pulled, the governor pulled the other way to ensure it did what it was designed to do, and that was to shut the engine down to avoid damage. Finally, we limped into Culloden Moor, and my aching arms and back could be rested. Control had already worked out that we must have been in trouble, due to the amount of time we had been in section. The 2200 shed men had made **27030** ready, to come and rescue us. As soon as it had been established that we had not derailed, the 27 was dispatched from Inverness, put on top of the now silent 26, and the whole train was on its way south no more than one hour behind schedule.

I was also using up a lot of annual leave at this time, to spend time with the Deltics before their imminent withdrawal in eight weeks' time. My last ECML trip came over the weekend of 30 November, by which time the game was almost up for these magnificent locomotives. Travelling back to Scotland behind **55010** on a Saturday night sleeper train, it dawned on me I could not bear to watch them die one by one, and therefore would take no further part on the circus until the last day, a strategy for which I have no regrets. As I watched Number 10 disappear off to Haymarket in a cloud of exhaust, I knew that I would probably never see her in active service again. With the Highland Mainline closed for the usual Sunday engineering works, it was home the long way round, via Aberdeen.

The last weeks of 1981 were played out in an air of gloom and impending change. The weather across most of the UK was appalling, with snow, sub-zero temperatures and frost all taking their toll on locomotive availability, the timetable and the morale of the staff. The last of the Deltics would soon be gone, the Woodhead route had closed, and locomotives with years of serviceable life in them were being hastily withdrawn and sent for scrap. Both the 40s and 25s were extremely rare visitors to Inverness. Class 47s now dominated the Highland Mainline and were becoming more frequent on the Aberdeen road, too. We were told by management that from the following May, Class 26s would be ousted from both the far North and Kyle line services, and a pool of Class 37 locomotives would replace them. For Highland railway men, this meant getting to know a new fleet, and bringing them up to our standard. History showed us that whenever we got somebody else's cast-offs, they were always the runts of the litter and invariably clapped out. The shadow of the new model business-led railway was being cast over us, and I did not like what I saw. My last footplate turn of 1981 involved a trip to Lairg and back with John Hay. I tried to convey my sense of impending doom to John, but as one of life's eternal optimists, he was having none of it. John's view was, "that which does not kill you will make you stronger," although to be frank, I remained far from convinced. Even as I drank strong tea, and listened to the gusty little Type 2 working hard in the weak, early-morning sunshine, my spirits remained low, and not for the first or last time, I wondered if I had made a mistake joining an industry in such terminal decline. I think even Jock was shocked when with very little notice, the smelter at Invergordon, which had only opened in 1971, closed towards the end of the year.

Alcan bought out British Aluminium, and for a whole bunch of reasons, deemed Invergordon to be uneconomic. As was typical with cold-hearted capitalists, the place closed with the loss of 700 jobs, just before Christmas. The scale of our loss was considerable: an annual 100k ton plus of freight north of Inverness dropped to 20k ton, at the stroke of a pen. More importantly, Invergordon was rendered a ghost town, and many people left, never to return. Queen and Davie Bowie may have been at the top of the charts, singing about being "under pressure", but in our contracting little world, we were feeling it.

JIMMY HELMSDALE AND 40061 CLIMB TO THE SLOCHD WITH A VERY HEAVY AFTERNOON GOODS IN 1981.

Chapter 3 - Flexible Rosters

The New Year dawned in sombre circumstances. Many of us had said our farewells for the last time at Kings Cross on Saturday 2 January, and a new lifestyle now beckoned. My love of railways had reached its peak, and everything now was downhill. I travelled home to Inverness behind **47455** on the 0840 from Edinburgh. Never again would I feel the tired satisfaction of an ECML Deltic-hauled overnight. I had previously arranged all of Sunday off, to allow me time to re-adjust my emotions, ahead of the next chapter in my life. The whole of the first week of 1982 was spent on shed and ferry work, other than a trip to Aberdeen and back with **27108** on Thursday. There would be no need to look out for the 0855 from Edinburgh today, as its motive power was of no real interest to me. The following week, weather conditions took a turn for the worse in the Highlands, and snow and harsh frosts played havoc with the timetable. On Sunday, Sandy Johnson and I were rostered to work the 0805 newspaper train to Lairg. We prepared our locomotive **26035**, only to be told we weren't leaving Inverness until 1135, so late was the connecting train containing all the Sunday papers from the south. 1S03 (the only Class 1 to run north of Inverness) was a big train for a Type 2, and with nine vans behind us, little time could be made up on our journey north.

The main off-loading point for newspaper traffic was Dingwall, Invergordon, Tain and Lairg. A fleet of vans and wholesalers were waiting for us at each stop. Bundles of papers were quickly unloaded and then taken by road to numerous towns and villages in a wide geographical area. On a day such as today, some of the villages on the west coast of Scotland would not get their papers until at least 1600 that afternoon. Out in the islands, it was even worse, with papers often not arriving until Monday morning. One of the perks of working this train was that the crew was given a bundle of papers to leaf through, while enjoying our tea break at Lairg. We were so late today that all we had time for at Lairg, was to run the locomotive round the stock, fill up our mash can and then head for home. Even now, our tribulations were not at an end, as **26035** threw in the towel at Alness with a complete loss of power, or LOP, as it was known. As Sandy settled down to read his paper, I set off into the biting cold wind to lay detonators and summon assistance.

In those days, the outer limit for protection was 1.25 miles, so a long walk lay ahead. After assistance had been sent for, you had to remain at this location and exhibit a red flag as the assisting engine arrived. This was a simple task that someone got so badly wrong in the Cruden Bay accident in 1977, when an assisting Class 40 had run into, and destroyed, the rear coach of the very train it was meant to be rescuing. Fortunately, **26046** was on her way back from a Kyle line ballast drop, so my wait, huddled in the bushes with my great-coat wrapped like a blanket around me, was relatively short, in comparison to waiting for rescue from Inverness. This coat was given to me by a retiring driver the winter before, and would keep me warm for the rest of my footplate career. In fact, I kept that coat right up to moving to Cardiff in 1990, when stupidly I decided to throw it out, along with many other items from my footplate days. It had got a bit damp, stored in my garage at Pegswood, so it felt like the right thing to do. If I had kept it, then I am certain it would still be wearable today. Back to 1982, the lone hoot from the approaching 26 ended my daydreaming, and as I climbed into the warm familiar cab, I mentally prepared myself for the barrage of jokes and insults from its crew. I wasn't disappointed. We finally arrived back in Inverness just before 1700, or four hours late against schedule.

Things fared little better the next day. Sandy and I were rostered to work the 1448 passenger service for Glasgow QS. When booking on duty, and much to my surprise, the foreman, Jock MacAngus, told us this train was cancelled, was coaching stock for the train had frozen brakes. In addition, our back working 1S59, the down *Clansman*, was reported as running over three hours late from Preston. Therefore, a set of Perth men would work this train, and go home passenger on the 2350 internal overnight from Inverness. A day in the mess room loomed, something which I would normally be unhappy about. However, with the weather set to get worse as night-time arrived, and the mercury plunging into minus double digits, a day in the warm began to hold some appeal. Of course, life never turns out quite as we would wish. Just after 1700, the mess room phone rang with a message for Sandy and I to take **26046** and go all speed towards Achnasheen. **26042** had hit a tree which had fallen onto the line, and was limping home with the 1710 from Kyle of Lochalsh. The rescued from the day before had now become the rescuers. We did indeed intercept **26042** at Achnasheen, and discovered the control and regulating air pipes on the buffer beam had become damaged, and with air being lost to atmosphere, only around 50% traction power was available. The climb up Glen Carron must have been very slow. Safely back in Inverness, we discovered that night's sleeper trains were being diverted via Aberdeen. Such was the ferocity of the storm blowing on Drumochter, the PW reported drifts of up to 15 feet in places. Our original train that evening, 1S59, finally arrived in Inverness just before midnight, after coming the long way round.

Our life was about to take another turn for the worse. The drivers' union ASLEF, led by Ray Buckton, had been in dispute for some time with the British Railways Board over the subject of flexible rostering. At the time, all footplate crews worked a maximum of an eight-hour day. Anything over and above that, such as the time incurred by the failure of **26035**, would be overtime, payable at enhanced rate. Under the new proposal, we would have a working day ranging from seven hours to nine hours. This would, in theory anyway, allow us to go further afield in our working day, and also take unproductive time out of the roster, on shorter trip and local passenger trains. In exchange for this flexibility, we would gain an additional day of annual leave and a 6% pay rise. The BRB saw flexible rostering as a must-have prize, to demonstrate to Thatcher and her government that a move away from steam age conditions was at last underway. To ASLEF, it was the thin end of the wedge, and any concessions now would lead to further erosion of hard-won rights for footplate staff, going back to the 1900s.

With the National Union of Railwaymen (NUR) already signing up to the new deal, the battle lines were drawn, and on 20 January we began the first of a series of two-day rolling strikes and overtime bans which would continue right through until the summer months. In combination with the weather, these strikes in January decimated freight traffic, and resulted in much of it being lost to the road network forever. Between 20 and 30 January, I only worked two revenue-earning turns of duty. Both involved special freight workings on the Highland Mainline with **47347** and **47052**. The situation carried on for most of February, and it was only when we entered the month of March that a temporary truce to hostilities was called, to allow further time for discussion. However, Thatcher turned the screw, by cutting the government grant to the industry, which some say resulted in the Advanced Passenger Train (APT) project being scrapped. The only real event of note for me on a personal basis in February was a trip to Aberdeen, with **25109** attached as pilot locomotive to the train engine of the 1444 Inverness to Aberdeen. With March proving to be strike-free, much freight traffic was moved across the whole network. Taking week commencing 14 March as an example, we took **27105/27212/27211/40034** and **47209** to Invergordon smelter, clearing out the remaining finished material, before the bulldozers moved in. The trip with the 40 on 18 March proved to be my last trip north of Inverness behind one of these fine machines. This class still put in sporadic appearances in Inverness, right up until 1984 and in the case of D200, up to 1986.

Of all the routes Inverness covered, the Far North and Kyle lines were my own favourites. Whenever possible, I tried to swop onto a turn which went north of Inverness. This was often easier said than done, as both Perth and Aberdeen work involved mileage payments, and the chance to earn some much-needed additional cash. These payments had their roots in the steam era, and in essence, incentivised crews to work over longer mileages, and in the case of the fireman, to shovel more coal –

anything up to eight tons per day through these big hills. Aberdeen trips brought an additional two hours per day pay, and Perth, two hours and 30 minutes. A useful addition to the pay packet, and if a bunch of mileage work came in the same week as a Sunday turn, your take home pay would be doubled.

One such week started with a shed turn on Sunday 21 March, then four nights to Perth with the up *Royal Highlander*, and returning home with the internal overnight from Glasgow and Edinburgh. *The Highlander* was still formed of duel heat Mark 1 stock at the time. The 47s we had that week were **47480**, **47464**, **47160** and **47274**. All trips were routine, other than the one with Haymarket's **47274** on the Friday. We had already seen the locomotive fail at Perth 24 hours earlier with low power, and both myself and Pat Macdonald, the driver, were somewhat surprised to see her steaming at the head of the 15-coach train the next evening. Looking at the repair book, we saw the infamous entry of NFF against the low power booking by the Eastfield driver. NFF stood for 'No Fault Found', and usually meant the fault was still present, ready to strike at any time. Pat gave me first drive, and as soon as the big brush got her nose into the climb to Culloden, it was obvious all was far from well. The amps were all over the place, and thick acrid smoke from the exhaust suggested unburnt fuel was passing to atmosphere. We staggered southwards, losing time on the uphill sections and making it up downgrade, as best we could. Arrival in Perth was only ten minutes adrift of schedule, and with no replacement locomotive available, the ailing 47 was sent away into the night towards Mossend. Such was the criticality of Type 4 power in Scotland at the time that it was doubtless dispatched back to Inverness on 1S07, the 2150 from Euston.

With the arrival of 37 power on the far north line only weeks away, it was a case of having one last hurrah with the superb Class 26 locomotives, which had dominated the route since the withdrawal of the 24s in the mid-1970s. I managed trips with **26030/35/39/41/42/43**, along with several others on the Kyle road. I also managed to avoid **37014**, which was the Inverness training locomotive, and based at the depot for many weeks for this purpose. While a handful of Inverness drivers already signed for this type of locomotive, the majority along with those at Wick, Kyle and Thurso, did not. In addition, all the fitting staff and electricians would have also required training, in preparation for the arrival of the Inverness eight to their new home. The training loco would usually work the mid-morning train to Wick when required. This allowed Inverness and Wick/Thurso men to have training on the EE machine.

For three nights commencing on 27 April, Jock Russell and I travelled passenger to Perth, to work the Dunbar cement back to Inverness. This was a huge train, with over 1,000 tons when fully loaded with its maximum number of PCA wagons. The motive power on all three trips was **27212** and **27111**, both displaced ex-E&G high-speed machines. With 2,500 horsepower on tap, this class of locomotive would haul the train up Drumochter at around 18mph, compared with the 12mph which could be expected from the booked 20s. The other advantage of a 27 was the propensity for 20s to suffer high water temperature while working these trains. This would result in an almost cast-iron certainty of arriving in

Inverness with one locomotive shut down, and the other one boiling and frothing away from overwork. I believe these machines only had a small water header tank containing 50 gallons, and any leaks in the system, combined with the many hours of full power hill-climbing, would be terminal.

None of the Inverness crews were sorry to see the back of the 20s, or 'thoosands', as we knew them. However, as is well documented elsewhere, by this time, the 27s had developed their own Achilles heel, in that fires in the control cubicles were on an upward trend. I remember once, the principle technical officer in Inverness showing me some wiring he had removed from the control cubicle of **27007**. The wiring was so old and brittle, it snapped like a twig when bent. This may have gone some way to explaining the demise of **27202**, which suffered a horrific fire while working one of the overnight freights to Inverness, one summer's evening in 1980. The control cubicle caught fire as the 27 struggled up the big hill near the Garry Bridge, and by the time Willie Cormack and Willie Birnie had been alerted to the conflagration behind them, by a passing lorry driver on the A9, the fire was sufficiently well alight to make on the onboard fire extinguishers unable to extinguish the flames. Despite assistance from the fire brigade at Blair Atholl, the locomotive was a write-off. Its burnt-out shell stood in the sidings at Dalwhinnie, waiting recovery, for many weeks afterwards. How the guard managed to sleep through the whole thing in the back cab, with a raging inferno six feet behind him, is still a mystery to me, all these years later. The gentleman concerned only awoke when Mr Birnie climbed into the back cab, and told him he was about to be barbecued.

I missed the launch of the summer timetable, and the challenge of running to time, on the far north line's accelerated schedules, as my health began to go rapidly downhill, following a week to Kyle with the 0655 mail service. I was dogged by problems, which I believe were caused by me returning to work too quickly, following my horrific accident in 1980. My first trip on the 37s came on 20 May, when Freddy Mason and I worked **37017** to Lairg on the 0615 from Inverness. Two days later it was **37035** to Brora on the 1110 service, returning with **37262** on the corresponding up train. What immediately struck me, apart from the almost impossibly tight schedules on certain stretches (management had optimistically shaved over 20 minutes off the overall journey time), was the hard ride of the 37 compared with the 26. They almost seemed to grind themselves round corners, and tear up the track on the straights. Later on, with the onset of autumn, we would also find out that they did not like climbing hills on leaf-covered rails. No end of trouble, delay and heart ache awaited us.

Further bouts of ill health, and a return of the flexible rostering dispute, deprived me of much of the early summer of 1982. Such was the debilitating nature of my illness that only a course of steroids, as prescribed by my doctor, gave any relief to my discomfort. Things came to a head when the then BR Chairman, Peter Parker, issued us all with a letter informing us that we would be dismissed without notice if we did not return to work immediately. In fact, between 12 June and 18 July, my only trip on the footplate was to Aberdeen and back with **27002**. The Chas and Dave classic "Down to Margate" remains a real earworm from that period of my life.

Upon my full return to work on 18 July, life and my health seemed better than they were for some time. Undoubtedly, the footplate community felt a great degree of bitterness about the manner in which we perceived we had been treated by the BRB, and its threat to close the whole network down, and dismiss us all without notice. This anger was directed at the small number of men who had defied the strike and carried on working. To trade unionists, they were 'scabs' and 'blacklegs'. To me, they just happened to be a bunch of enginemen who thought for themselves, and had a different view to the majority. The one issue I could be critical on is that they never had the strength of character to tell us up front, and the reasons why they would be working. Sneaking in to work through the back gate probably caused as much anger as coming to work in the first place. A friend of mine, who was based at Saltley depot in Birmingham in 1982, had the courage to attend the ASLEF branch meeting and tell them he would be coming to work and why. Although still a 'scab', I know from others involved that he gained a degree of respect for this alone. Not that I can imagine anyone daring to call the giant of a street-fighting man a 'scab' to his face, unless extremely brave or stupid.

With so much freight clogging up the system following the two-week shutdown, all hands to the pumps were required, to get things moving again. This gave me the opportunity to enjoy trips over the Highland line with **40167** and **25239**, as traffic from Invergordon was moved south. Also, we took **37017** to Brora, dropping off household coal at several rural yards along the way. On the return, we collected empty oil tanks from Lairg. We even went to Evanton with **26038**, to collect several wagons of scrap from the Graham Wood private siding there. This was my only trip to this location, before the track was removed a few years later. Evanton was situated between Alness and Dingwall. It gave access to an industrial yard and had a single set of south-facing points controlled by a ground frame, operated by the guard. Any traffic entering the yard would first have to be tripped to Invergordon, to enable the locomotive to run round, before heading back south. This enabled the wagons to be propelled into the siding and left for collection at a later date, once they had been fully loaded with scrap. Between Dingwall and Tain, five such locations existed, but little logic seemed to apply to how they operated. Evanton and Fearn were south-facing junctions, while Invergordon Smelter, distillery and MK Shands were north-facing. This made visiting them all in one day hugely complex, and it was not unusual to have the locomotive sandwiched between rakes of wagons fore and aft, as we shuttled between sites.

Jimmy Helmsdale and I booked on one Saturday to work to Aberdeen, only to find our booked locomotive **26039** had failed with flat batteries, and wouldn't start. Jimmy sent me back to see the duty foreman, Adam Sutherland, to see what replacement power was available, as our 26 would need a good few hours on the depot's battery charger, before any hope of a successful start-up. As Adam pored over his engine sheet, I was fully expecting him to say, "have 27 this, or 47 that". I did a double take when Adam said, "take **40124** from the wagon shops". I could hardly believe my luck! Jimmy was always good for a drive, and I enjoyed an unexpected and impromptu spin with the split box veteran. The locomotive was, I believe, based at Gateshead at the time, and must have worked its way north via a series of freights. While doing my research for this book, I noted that the locomotive was withdrawn in early 1984, and cut up the same year, thus making my trip with her even more poignant. With 2,000 horsepower on tap, and only five coaches, we flew across the top and had another early arrival in Aberdeen. Whatever the reason for it being in Inverness, someone must have wanted it back, as on arrival at Aberdeen, a set of Ferryhill shed men awaited to take our 40 off us and to give us **26034**, as a more suitable form of traction for the return trip. More good fortune shone on me the following week, when Stan Paton and I had **37183,** and later in the week, **26042/46**. On Highland mainline passenger jobs, both were rare catches in this rapidly changing world. It was fantastic to be back in the cab of a Type 2, running at speed on a Class 1 service. A good pair seemed perfect to me for just about any job thrown at them, and with only a few hundred horsepower less than a 47, they were well capable of running to time if driven hard, and in the style Inverness men were known for.

In what was rapidly becoming a whole month of firsts, and in some cases lasts, Willie Finlayson and I took **26042** down the Inverness harbour branch on a track recovery train on 23 and 24 August. The once extensive network of lines within the harbour complex was being reduced, to make way for further expansion of the Longman industrial estate. It was sad to see disused track being ripped out for ever, and gave me another reality attack, after the highs of the previous few weeks. The harbour branch is long gone now, and only a few rusty relics remain of this fascinating piece of infrastructure. A far cry from the days of it having its own shunting engine, as crews spent the whole of their eight hours shift shunting the harbour, and still not getting all the work done.

This Indian summer still had one last surprise in store for me, and that came during the week commencing 19 September. Somehow, I had managed to pick up five mileage turns to Perth, and a Sunday off 2000 spare, so a bumper pay packet loomed the following week. On the Sunday I spent a pleasant and informative day with dear old Bert Ross, relaying Platform 5 with **26042** and tripping the recovered rail out to Millburn Yard. Bert and the guard, Brian Leech, were in good form, and the supervisor in charge of the work gave us permission to adjourn to the railway staff club adjacent to Platform 7, for a liquid lunch. As soon as the day's work was over, we returned to the club for a good session, and some pool. I finally made for home around 2200 hours, with most of my day's earnings already spent on the 'demon drink'. With my next turn of duty not until 2150, plenty of recovery time lay ahead.

My driver for the following week was the legend, Kenny Campbell – small in stature, but huge in presence. Kenny was an excellent engineman, other than when he was in a bad mood. He liked to travel light, and his kit consisted of a standard railway issue bardic lamp, and a green teacup liberated from some buffet car or other. You never saw Kenny carrying a bag unless he was going on holiday. His view was that bags just contained stuff you never really needed out on the road, and a driver should know how to fix his locomotive, without referring to charts and manuals. On the first night, we had **47550** as our motive power – a surprising choice for a 35mph vacuum-braked train. We soon discovered the brush was heading south for tyre turning, and therefore had a 45mph speed restriction in force, and would no doubt have been 'T coded' to this effect in TOPS, by the lads in control. This 47 had been allocated to Inverness since 1976, and along with **47472** and **47546**, formed the backbone of the fleet allocated to the *Clansman,* on paper at least. However, **47550** always had a bit of a reputation at the depot, as being the jinx loco. It was forever blowing pistons and cylinder liners, plus a few accidents took place to fitters working on it. Every depot had a jinx, and this was ours. The big brush made light work of the 500-ton train, and we arrived in Perth with time in hand. Our return working, which was the 6N01 Millerhill to Inverness Class 6 goods, was already in the yard waiting for us. A quick fill of the mash can, and then we climbed aboard **25282** for the run north, back in Millburn Yard by 0530, and on shed for 6am.

This pattern continued all week, with trips with **40002/37014/27210/27204/25230/37028** and **25072** making for a variable and enjoyable week. On the Tuesday evening, we still made it all the way to Perth, despite **40002** hauling a dead **08753** en route to works in Glasgow. The speed for the dead haul of a 08 was 25mph, so we enjoyed a sedate and leisurely trip south. The week is also remembered as being my own personal swansong with Class 25s in the Highlands. It was the last time that I would work on three different ones in the same week, and on the Saturday morning Kenny allowed me to drive **25072** all the way home. It was nice to feel the little engine working hard, and we climbed over the mountains with a relatively light train weight-wise, and timed at 60mph as an added bonus. On several occasions, we ran down and caught **47107** working the internal overnight, such was our progress, as the 'Flyer' lived up to its name. This pleased Kenny, as he was keen to get on shed by 5am, and home for a few hours' sleep, as he had a darts match later that day. As for me, with a rest day Saturday to look forward to, it was home to bed and then out spending the money I had earned that week. Although in the context of historical accuracy, I did also purchase a new Dawes racing bike. A life-changing moment, as it started a passion for cycling which continues to this day.

With flexible rostering now accepted by most of the Inverness footplate crews, life began to feel stable again, and we continued to provide the best possible service we could to our paying passengers and freight customers. Our roster comprised a 56-man main roster, split into eight week blocks of work, a four-man shed and ferry roster, a four-man passenger and goods yard shunting link, and then a one-man roster for Willie Calder, a diabetic, who permanently worked our 0630-1400 preparation turn. The driver's assistants' roster mirrored the main driver roster, other than you no longer worked with the same driver for weeks on end. With single manning becoming an accepted practice in the Highlands, drivers and their assistants found themselves carrying out different work, and perhaps not seeing each other for several weeks at a time.

Following the end of hostilities between ASLEF and the BRB, freight traffic continued to decline, although on the trains that did remain, tonnages seemed high. By this time, we had lost most freight traffic on the north and west lines. Burghead and Dufftown only operated on an as-required basis, most goods yards had all but closed, and the only wagon-load traffic which remained viable was household coal and the seasonal potato flow. The Invergordon gas tanks had ceased running and the whisky distillery, while still receiving rail traffic, only did this on an as-required basis. The finished product now left exclusively by road. Tar to Culloden and cement for Inverness remained healthy, as did the seasonal rock salt traffic from Winsford in Cheshire. Fuel oil to Lairg ran on a regular twice-weekly basis, as did whisky tanks to Keith and Elgin. This was nothing like the railway I had joined, and unbeknown to me, nothing like the railway which was still to come.

Fortunately, with road access so poor to many parts of the Highlands and Islands, our passenger flows remained healthy, with overcrowding and subsequent relief trains needed on the Highland Line in high summer. We still held the contract to move newspapers, with the Lairg train loading heavily every Sunday, and additional vans being carried on the early morning Far North and Kyle trains every weekday.

On the Perth road, Class 47s hauling the early pressure-ventilated Mark 2 coaching stock was now the norm, and slowly, they were making their presence felt more and more, also over the top to Aberdeen. English Electric Class 37s now virtually dominated the Far North line, and the Class 26s still held sway on the Kyle road, and would continue to do so for another year at least.

1982 ended with further drama, and another challenge to test the versatility of Inverness footplate staff. With the onset of autumn, the 37s began to show up as being totally unsuitable to maintain adhesion on the hills of the Far North. It was not uncommon for trains to be delayed by 60 minutes or more, due to the struggling 37's wheels slipping on wet and damp leaves. So much damage was being done to the locomotive wheel sets that something had to be done. The answer was, of course, that if the new doesn't work, then bring back the old. An instruction was issued that the first and last trains of the day must be operated with a combination of 26/37 traction, and that the 26 should be leading heading north whenever possible. My first taste of this eclectic mix came on Thursday 21 October, when Peter Mackenzie and I had **26035** and **37261** to Brora on the 1720 down, returning with **26024** and **37017** on the last train of the day into Inverness. With the 26 dropping sand to help the bigger loco at the back, the climbs out of Dingwall, Lairg and Dunrobin all seemed much easier, if not totally slip-free. This new combination proved a winning one, so long as the 26 had its sand boxes kept full and dry. Almost overnight, the problem went away.

THE VIEW FROM 26034 AS ITS TOPS CORRIEMULLE ON A FREEZING FEBRUARY MORNING IN 1981.

TYPE 2'S GALORE. 26035 SITS IN NUMBER 2 SHED ROAD SURROUNDED BY A CLASS MATE AND A 27.

THE OFFICE 1. 26034 AT KYLE OF LOCHALSH IN FEBRUARY 1981.

THE OFFICE 2. 26042 HAS A BREATHER AT ACHNASHEEN LATER THE SAME YEAR.

Peter Queen and I were crewing **47001** on the 1240 to Aberdeen on a routine Wednesday lunchtime. I was in the driving seat, running along at 65mph, with time in hand, reflecting on the day thus far. Rounding the long sweeping right hand curve on the approach to Inverurie, I suddenly noticed Peter had fallen onto the cab floor, and was clearly in great pain. Stopping a mile short of the station was in no one's interest, so I made the decision to keep going. As soon as we stopped at the station, I flew out of the seat to check on his welfare. He kept pointing at some pills in his bag and was mumbling that he needed them double quick. By this time, the guard was knocking at the door to find out why nobody was looking back for his tip to go. "Tell the station staff to get an ambulance in Aberdeen!" I said, "and hold on to your hat". I drove like the wind to Aberdeen, all the time looking at Peter lying on the floor, curled up and clearly in great distress. As we ran down Platform 6 several minutes early, a sea of relief swept over me, as the welcome sight of a waiting ambulance crew came into view. They had Peter off the engine, and onto a stretcher, before the wheels had stopped turning. Elation turned to panic, when I realised that I had driven for over 13 miles on my own, even though not yet passed for driving, along with liberally interpreting some of the line speeds, too.

Following the Peter Queen incident, I kept waiting for someone in authority to say something to me. As each day passed, I became more confident that nothing was going to be said. I guess the powers-that-be had decided that if they pretended the incident never took place, then it would be a case of "least said, soonest mended". Thankfully, Peter made a full recovery, and was back with us by the end of the year.

My earworm for the year was Rod Stewart's number 1 hit *Baby Jane*, which appeared to be played at every bar, nightclub and radio station that summer. The opening line is 'Baby Jane, don't keep me hanging on the line' – the perfect song for the Burghead branch. One area of the operation which still seemed unaffected by the recession and cutbacks was our track-relaying and ballast programme. Every weekend saw a large job somewhere on the patch, with both the Highland and Aberdeen lines having money spent on them. Even north of Inverness, work would take place periodically. I can't say that I ever saw Sir Peter Parker's "crumbling edge of quality" have a tangible impact. To service all this work, we had a crew book on a 0700 and 1225, Monday to Friday, to work as required across the patch. On a Saturday, we had two 2000 turns for engineering purposes, and then any amount of Sunday turns needed to complete the work.

As a general principle, the weekday jobs were to collect material needed at the weekend, or to remove waste from an earlier weekend job. This could be rails, sleepers or old ballast. Although, to be fair, it was not unheard-of on a weekday to go and drop some ballast or rails, but very much on an as-required basis. The driver for the morning permanent way turn, or trip H6, as it was known, was either Alistair Moore or Joe Polson, both of whom were medically restricted to the hours they worked. One of the many memories I have of Joe is that occasionally he would bring a whole, freshly cooked crab to have as his mid-morning snack. We sat in a siding, having our break, while Joe devoured his salty white meat, leaving an ever-increasing pile of shell to be disposed of, once we set sail again. He often offered me a piece of crab meat, and told me how good it was for me. I always politely declined, and stuck to my more traditional cheese or ham roll.

The motive power for the weekday ballast diagrams was typically a Class 26 or 27; with most of the work being local, and the wagons vacuum brake-fitted, a Type 2 was ideal. Occasionally, this turn would throw up a 37 or 47 off-exam that needed a test run. However, this was very much the exception. I do recall one day being given a solo **20159** light to Elgin in order to pick up some ballast wagons. I was really looking forward to my nose-first Class 20 trip, until my driver Pat decided he was not driving the locomotive, as the guard had nowhere to sit while running light. Not that the guard was that bothered, but Pat was a real stickler for the manning agreements at that time.

Looking at a typical week on H6, we did the following:

- **Monday**: **26031** light engine to Blair Atholl to bring empty wagons from the weekend back to Inverness.

- **Tuesday**: **26024** (on test) failed at Kingussie with a traction motor flashover.

- **Wednesday**: **27107,** empty timber wagons to Carrbridge, went light to Kingussie, collected seven loads of ballast for Moy and then home light.

- **Thursday**: **26041**, light to Kingussie, three loads of ballast to Dalwhinnie, light to Blair Atholl and then worked a train of long welded rails to Inverness

- **Friday**: **26030**, light to Aviemore to assist **27012,** which had failed on a goods train.

The trip with **26041** was memorable, as we had to bring 500 tons of rails to Inverness with only the engine and van brake. This was one of the last times I ever remember working a Class 9 (fully unbraked freight). The driver, Peter Queen, allowed me to drive under close supervision. At both the hill tops into Tomatin and Inverness, we stopped, and asked the guard to apply a requisite number of hand brakes on the wagons, before gingerly making our descent at no more than 20 mph. At the bottom of the hill, it was brakes off, and then carry on as normal for a while, or until the next place AWB was needed. I must admit, my palms were sweaty, especially on the descent for Culloden to Inverness. By this time, all the brake blocks were hot and smoking, and therefore less effective.

We had in our mind the runaway of a similar train, a year or so earlier, when only the quick thinking of the signaller prevented a huge pile-up. An unbraked freight was on the descent to Inverness when the driver lost control. Speed soon picked up to 60 mph, and possibly even more. The train emerged from under the A9 flyover at Raigmore, with the brakes looking like Catherine Wheels and the 'train in distress' being sounded on the horn. The signaller at Millburn Junction, who was obviously on the ball, sent the train running away in right direction code 4-5-5 to the box in advance at Welshes Bridge, who in turn set the points away from Platform 1 of the station towards Rose Street. With nothing running on the north line at the time, the errant train was passed on to Clachnaharry, and the runaway given safe passage through the station area and onto the Rose Street curve. The train finally came to rest alongside the Beauly Firth, a good mile or so beyond its intended stopping point.

During this autumn period, I also had my first Class 37 on the Kyle road. On Saturday 9 September, Jimmy Smith and I were required for duty at 0554, to work the 0655 Inverness to Kyle and 1108 return. Presenting myself at the booking on window, I was expecting to be told the location of our Class 26 for the train, and had the pleasant surprise of being told our motive power for the day was to be **37262**. Jimmy arrived a few minutes behind me, and it was obvious he was unwell and suffering from an early winter cold, or something else picked up the previous evening. I could detect he was not happy at the prospect of a day in the cab of a 37, and would have much preferred the comfort of a Type 2 instead. To his credit, he said nothing, and just got on with things. "Are you happy to drive all day, mate?" he asked, which of course I was. I filled the tea can while Jimmy made ready the locomotive for the trip west. Our train was in its customary Platform 7, and after dropping down to put the shackle and pipes on, I opened the steam valve to begin putting a steady flow of steam through the short train.

The winter Kyle formation was three vehicles, made up of 2 TSOs and a BG, giving a train weight of 105 tons tare – nothing for a Type 3 loco. Returning to the cab from the boiler compartment, I noticed Jimmy had made our tea, and was settled down in the right-hand seat with his Daily Record. The run to Dingwall was no different to anything I had previously experienced on far north turns. However, as we swung west, it immediately became apparent how the 37 ground its way around the corners, as opposed to the smooth ride of a smaller machine. The climb of the Ravens Rock was no better than with a Type 2. Once the 20mph restriction at Achterneed was passed, it was a case of piling on the amps, and letting the locomotive settle in for the remainder of the climb. However, with a 37, it was more a case of finding a power setting that worked, and it required constant tinkering to maintain the road speed at 35 mph.

Once over the top, in the deep rock gorge, we rumbled down to Garve, with the 37 grinding its way along the shores of the loch of the same name. Station duties involved off-loading several bags of mail and newspapers, before tackling the next climb up to Loch Luichart. More slipping and sliding up the wooded valley contributed to my feeling of unease, and displeasure with the performance of the EE machine. I longed for the steady beat of a 26 doing what it did best, and had done effortlessly for the last 20 years. With no passengers at either request stop along this section, we made good time to Achnasheen, and our crossing with the 0710 from Kyle, which, of course, had its usual headlight fitted and steaming Class 26. This train was worked by a Kyle crew, and on this occasion the driver was the infamous SPAD, a man known throughout the whole of the Highlands for his Jack Dee-like expressions, and absence of a sense of humour.

With more mail and papers unloaded, we made light work of the climb to the summit at Luib, before another headlong plummet downhill to sea level at Strathcarron. The hardest part of the trip now lay ahead. With a 26 you would leave Strathcarron on notch 2, and let the gradient drive you along the shores of Loch Carron to Stromeferry. With a line speed of only 25 mph along here, this driving technique would ensure the speed was kept between 20-30 mph. The uphill sections would see speed tail off, and on the next downhill, speed would increase again. It may sound easy, but it was a real art form, and one of the most difficult roads that I have ever driven over.

Goodness only knows how the drivers of today manage it, with the all-seeing black box monitoring every move. However, back to 1982, we had passengers for Attadale, and also at the small station of Duncraig, serving the girls' boarding school. With further stops at Stromeferry, Plockton and Durnish, we finally arrived in Kyle on time at 0940. Most Inverness crews had a fairly standard procedure, to maximise the layover time in Kyle. While the mail was still being unloaded, we ran the engine round and backed it up against the stock. As soon as the guard gave us the tip that station duties had been completed, the stock was pushed back into position for departure at 1108, before shutting the locomotive down, and heading for the small mess room. While a pot of steaming tea was brewing, the guard joined us with a bundle of newspapers, and we settled down to enjoy a late breakfast and some banter about what ever happened to be topical, or the fortunes of one of the local football teams. Around 1040 or thereabouts, one of us went outside to crank up the locomotive and turn on the boiler, to begin to heat the train for the 82-mile trip home.

For me, the last few minutes were always spent with a short walk along the harbour wall, to take in the stunning views of Skye and the magnificent Cuillen ridge beyond. Departure at 1108 was invariably prompt, and after picking up small numbers of passengers at intermediate stations, we would arrive in Achnasheen on time, to await the arrival of the second westbound train of the day. What followed was usually a fast run home to Inverness, with an arrival in Platform 5 just before 1400. The 1400 disposal crew took the locomotive for fuel and water, and we walked to the shed, and booked off duty at 1410. This gave plenty of time on a Saturday afternoon to watch a match, have a few beers, or go home for a sleep, if a heavy night on the town lay ahead.

The year still held a few final surprises for me, and the first one came on Thursday 25 November. Willie Macdonald and I booked on at 2150 to work the 2222 goods to Perth, returning with the 0150 Perth to Inverness. I was thrilled to find the locomotive for the trip south was to be none other than **40167**. We had a pleasant trip south with the ageing whistler, and as an added bonus, I drove the whole way. Arriving in Perth NY just before 1am, we had a leisurely 50 minutes to rest, before the long trek north. The yard supervisor told us our train was on time, and would arrive in the yard just after 0130. After taking tea, and being largely ignored by the Perth men, who were more often than not ambivalent to us Highlanders, we walked out into the cool night air. This resulted in a further double-take, as the disc eyes of another 40 approached us.

40069 was our power home. How long was it since I had enjoyed a 40 both ways on the mainline? A long time, and this was to be the last time. It was such a thrill to feel the hard, steady rumble of the 133-ton Healey Mills machine, as she effortlessly ploughed northwards, with a train weighing almost 600 tons. I sat back, and allowed the sensations of sound, power and the warmth of the cab embrace me, as I savoured every minute of the trip. I knew very well that tonight, fate had dealt me a hand that was unlikely ever to be repeated. As we walked away from the 40, after depositing it safely on the fuel road, it was impossible to resist a backwards glance at the work-stained and grime-encrusted outline of the whistler. I thought I had possibly had my last trip on a 40 for the year, and with the ever-increasing influx of 47s, it might be some time until I heard the reassuring sound again. In fact, my next 40 trip came on Sunday 12 December, when Freddie Mason and I booked on at the unearthly hour of 2am, to relieve the previous evening's night shift, on a track relaying job at Tomatin. As soon as I stepped out of the Land Rover that had taken us to site, the flute-like whistle of a 40 told me that once again, my luck was in. Walking the line towards the viaduct, the huge bulk of **40085** appeared out of the gloom. The cab light was on, and I climbed into Number 2 end of the 40. However, the job itself proved to be a real anti-climax. We did not move one inch, from 0230 until 0900, when it was our turn to be relieved by the set of men who would finish the job, and ensure the line was clear to reopen at 1300.

My second surprise was a trip to Aberdeen with a grubby **37112** on 20 December. Inverness was desperately short of steam heat power, and the Eastfield machine was in town, between freight workings. On Christmas Eve, I went to Perth and back with **47461** and **47423,** as an eventful year drew to a close, quietly and without drama. On the eve of New Year itself, Dan Wares and I went to Aberdeen and back with **26039,** booking off at 2353.

My total foot plate mileage for the year stood at 22,458, and ended with a whisky in the running foreman's office, with Dan, John Robertson the TCS, and a couple of the night shift maintenance staff. My notes tell me, that after Elgin, the only people aboard the 2040 were me, the driver and the guard. Without sounding stereotypical, most Scotsmen and women were off doing what we all did best at this time of year.

The second full year of life after Deltics started much as the first had ended, with a cold easterly wind, coupled with harsh frosts at night. My first turn of duty was not until Monday 3 January, when Joe Polson and I worked the southbound *Clansman* to Perth, with our own **47464** hauling twelve very well-filled coaches. This was normally a Perth turn, but with no inbound overnight the previous evening, it became a supplementary Inverness diagram, with Joe and I booked to take duty at 0945. On the return from Perth, we manned **47467** as pilot engine to **47472** on the 1322 from Edinburgh. This was to balance the electric train heat locomotive position in Inverness, for the two southbound London overnights later that evening. With over 6,000 horsepower for only six vehicles, we made light work of the trip home, and unsurprisingly stood waiting time at most stations.

The following day proved just as eventful. Initially, I was rostered as 0600 disposal, but around 0750, Willie Mackenzie, or 'The Professor' (as he was better known) and I were commandeered to take **26044**, and go all speed to Durnish. **26043** had failed there while working the 0700 from Kyle, and the Road to the Isles was blocked until rescue arrived. The locomotive and stock from the 0655 Inverness to Kyle had terminated at Strathcarron, and reformed the first train back to Inverness. Our job was to push the dead 26 and stock back to Kyle, and form the 1108 back to Inverness, hauled by **26044**. Thanks to some good old-fashioned teamwork, and a fast run with our rescue locomotive, we managed to achieve a right time departure of 2K14. I must add that failure of these machines was extremely rare. However, due to the very remote nature of the line, any failures resulted in considerable delay and inconvenience to our passengers.

The weather took a turn for the worse towards the middle of the month. Overnight on the 13th, Pat Macdonald and I had a really difficult and heavily delayed trip to Perth and back. On the way home with **47268,** we ploughed our way through some hefty drifts on Drumochter, and by the time we eventually arrived in Inverness, the stock looked as if it had just arrived from Greenland, and not Glasgow.

On 28 January, my old friend Jock Hay and I were booked 0400 spare, with no job. This involved a young fellow having to get out of his bed at 0300, and cycle into work through the empty streets, to then sit in the mess room, bored and clock-watching until home time. At 0545, the supervisor, Adam Sutherland, told us to take **26032** from the stores road, and to pilot **37262** on the 0615 to Wick. **37260** on the 0600 up from Wick was low on fuel, and we were to pilot it home in case of further problems. By the time we dropped on top of the 37 at Lairg, the fuel tank was all but empty, and the decision was made to shut down the 37, and let Jock and I do all the work with the 26. Despite a load of seven coaches, and a dead 37, the 'wee injun' did us proud, and lost no further time on schedule, during the 67-mile run home. **26032** with Jock at the controls performed superbly, and it was a case of rolling back the years for this gutsy little 26.

On Thursday 3 February, a routine trip to Aberdeen for my good friend Andrew Gardener turned into tragedy. The 'Cobbler' and his driver, Joe Polson, had enjoyed an incident-free trip to Aberdeen, and were returning home with the Class 27-hauled 1350 Aberdeen to Inverness. Running at 70 mph, passing Llanbryde near Elgin, a broken fishplate left a gap in the rail, and as a consequence, the rear Mark 2a coach derailed, and was dragged for 300m on its side. Sadly, a passenger travelling in the vehicle was killed, and three others had serious, but not life-threatening, injuries. The whole depot had a sombre feel to it for several days afterwards, as nobody could help but be affected by a loss of life on our railway. These events were thankfully few and far between, but nonetheless, we were forever vigilant.

A week or so later, and a fierce snowstorm hit the Highlands. Booking on for 1400 spare, I was immediately told to go with driver Willie Loban and take **26042** to patrol between Dalwhinnie and Blair Atholl. The logic was: our snowplough-fitted 26 would prevent the drifts from closing the line, until the large, independent snow ploughs had come back from ploughing the far north lines. The Type 2 rocked and swayed as we hit drifts of up to two feet deep in places. The plan was to plough the up line for the 1445 to Edinburgh, and plough the down line ahead of the late-running 1310 from Glasgow, before making a final trip ahead of the 1630 from Inverness, and the down *Clansman*. We returned to Inverness, and left the 26 on the fuel road, before finally booking off duty at 2030.

The big independent ploughs had returned onto the depot for fuel, before a night of doing battle with the big hills to the south. The following night, I was rostered to work the 2030 Inverness to London Euston, and back home from Perth with the 0110 internal overnight. While some of the snow had abated, we had some nasty weather to deal with, and as a consequence, we ran slightly late all evening. On the way back from Perth, we had **47160** for power. The 47 coped admirably with the big train and the weather, but the same cannot be said for its steam heating boiler. The flaky spanner steam heat generator could barely maintain 25psi of steam. For those poor souls aboard, it must have been a cold journey. Jim, or 'Flash', as we all knew him, was in quite a distressed state for the welfare of his passengers, and decided we should turn off the cab heating, in sympathy with those in the long rake of Mark 1 coaches behind. This altruistic behaviour only lasted until Dalwhinnie, by which time the windscreen had begun to freeze on the inside and prevent 'Flash' from seeing the road ahead. So, all the heaters were turned back on, and at last I began to thaw out.

Jim Macmillan was one of the stranger drivers at the depot. He very much kept his own counsel, and at times, seemed as if he lived in a world of his own. Despite this, he was an excellent mate, always good for a drive, and looked after you. I miss him, and will always remember him fondly.

Following a quiet and mundane few weeks, on Friday 1 April, Davie Fraser was my driver, and the two of us were rostered to work the 1230 Inverness to Glasgow as far as Perth, before returning with the down *Clansman*. Unusually, we managed to score with 'Generator' 47s both ways. We had the pioneer of the fleet, **47401,** on the outward leg, before returning home with **47410**. These engines may not have been everyone's cup of tea, but nobody could doubt that they were versatile. This type of 47 wasn't a stranger to our patch, but to have two on the same day must have been somewhat rarer.

With the commencement of the summer timetable, noticeable inroads were being made into our Highland Mainline passenger volumes, both by Stagecoach of Perth, and by Scottish Citylink coaches. The quality of the vehicles had improved massively, and with the A9 trunk road in much better shape than ever before, journey times were comparable, certainly in the case of leisure travel.

BR, to their credit, met this new challenge head-on with some aggressive marketing, and by launching its own bargain basement-priced Fridays-only, Glasgow to Inverness limited-stop *Jacobite* service. The train was formed of the Edinburgh to Glasgow spare set, and was therefore booked to be hauled by a Class 47/7 and DBSO. As Inverness had not been trained on DBSOs, the northbound and southbound service, which left Inverness at 1820 for Glasgow, had to be worked by Perth crews both ways. The train was an immediate success, and would often arrive or depart packed to the rafters, full of passengers enjoying a flat £5 fare to any station the train served, including Glasgow Queen Street.

As spring turned to summer, I slowly worked my way through the link, and slowly watched the older drivers retire, one by one. JG Munro, Alex Waters and Robert Blaney all retired, and poor old Ian Grant died in service. This did, of course, allow a good number of the senior passed men, such as Ronnie Donaldson, John Low and Frank (Biff) Boyd, to finally be made up to drivers on a permanent basis.

The relentless eradication of the old railway continued without mercy, and by July we no longer saw vacuum brake freight trains on a regular basis, as BR no longer carried wagon load coal to the area. Sidings up and down the Highland line, North road and out towards Elgin became surplus to requirements, and slowly rusted into terminal decay. In addition, the elimination of brake vans reduced the role of the goods guard to that of a mere travelling shunter. Many guards were more than happy with this arrangement, and saw an opportunity to sit in a nice warm cab, sleeping or reading between duties, as a step forwards. Older hands, such as Willy Flood and Donnie Leach, saw this as the thin end of the wedge, leading to the total elimination of guards in the future. They were scoffed at as pessimists, but how right they were.

With single-manning now taking hold on the Highland mainline, a virtual monopoly for Class 47s on the Aberdeen road, 37s dominating the Wick services and Class 26/37 to Kyle, much of the variety of the past had gone. So much so that I stopped writing down each locomotive we had on a daily basis, and only made notes in my diary for exceptional events. The odd surprise could still be found on the remaining freights, and in September, I was rostered a week on nights with one of the more infamous drivers, known to one and all as 'Cherry'. Our job involved booking on at 1900, to work the 1950 goods to Dunkeld, before changing cabs with Perth men on the northbound.

Over the course of the week, we had 2 x 20. **40158** (twice), **37292** (twice), and on the last night we came home with an ex works **37011**. All was well as we begin the climb out of Blair Atholl, with our 600-ton plus train. Speed balanced at around 18mph – not untypical for such a load. As the gradient stiffened to 1:72 above Struan, our speed fell back to 15mph, as the 37 dug in, with the worst of the climb still ahead. As we came off the reverse curves above Garry Bridge, the control circuit breaker (CCB) tripped, and we were plunged into darkness, as the now silent and electrically dead 37 quickly came to a halt. The traction manual for this class allowed no more than three resets, as this circuit breaker protected many of the main electrical circuits fitted on the power side of the locomotive. 'Cherry' liberally interpreted this as us having three goes each, and therefore that would make six in total! However, on every occasion the power handle was opened, it was accompanied by a loud bang and a total engine shut down. Even the ever-cheerful 'Cherry' admitted defeat, and following a quick confab with the guard, we decided assistance would be required.

Donnie Leech was to lay detonators to the rear, while I would do the front, before walking forwards to the line side telephone at the 42.5 milepost. This was the first time I had to lay detonators since the failure at Alness the previous year, and my first time during the hours of darkness. Walking out into the dark night, with only the light from my bardic lamp to guide me, was slightly eerie. Before long, I got the distinct impression that I wasn't alone, and it wasn't only my feet crunching on the ballast. The faster I walked, the faster my pursuer followed. I felt genuine fear. A walk soon became a run, and I was afraid to turn around, to see what monster might be following me in such a lonely place, especially after all the ghost stories from old Bert Ross. My fear turned to terror as something began to breath heavily very close behind me. I dropped the lamp, and I was away into the night.

Collapsing into a heap further up the line, I was both surprised and relieved to discover that I was now alone. I could see the faint glow of my lamp in the four foot, so retraced my steps, to discover a large red deer looking at me out of the darkness. My lamp had obviously attracted him down off the hill, and he had decided to follow me along the line. My slowly improving heart rate suddenly went into an alarming rate of positive climb, as my ears were alerted to the growl of an approaching 37.

Cherry had remembered the guard hadn't had his three attempts of resetting the CCB, so on his return from laying detonators, a further (this time successful) attempt was made to resurrect the locomotive. With the guard now back on board, and buoyed with new-found optimism, he took it upon himself to set off in pursuit of me, with his now healthy engine. I stood waving frantically, as the big engine bore down on me, with all lights, including the cab, illuminated. Just as I felt sure I was going to be abandoned in the night, the brakes went on, and I climbed aboard into the warm, welcoming cab environment. I must admit I did point out to him that the rules and regulations were quite clear: once a train had been declared a failure, then signalman's permission must be obtained before moving again. He just shrugged and said rules in these hills are just a guide, and not definitive, which came as a bit of a surprise to me. Then again, it was only a few years previously that I had been told that speed boards were also only a guide, so perhaps this magical kingdom I had joined had more to it than first met the eye. Cherry didn't push his luck, though, and we stopped at the first signal and told the box that we had left detonators in the rear of us, and asked for assisting engine to be sent to meet us at Aviemore.

I told the story some weeks later to Jock Hay, who was in hysterics at the thought of me running for my life in the night, as my driver chased me down with his no-longer broken-down train.

Another difficult autumn followed on the far north lines, with single Class 37s still proving unable to haul the heaviest trains unassisted, and once again requiring the 26/37 combination, to keep time and prevent wheel set damage on the EE machines. On the odd occasion, when a 37 had to work alone, no end of trouble took place, particularly on the standing start from Golspie along the four-mile climb to Dunrobin. One day, **37035** was slipping so badly that the driver jammed in the locomotive's wheel slip relay, to ensure we didn't stall on the bank. The 37 was hammered without mercy to make it over the hill, and without the all-important wheel slip protection, damage must have taken place to tyres or axles. However, desperate times meant desperate measures, and with assistance so far away, the job was kept running, albeit it a considerable cost. On another occasion, we couldn't get away from Golspie with the last train of the day, so the driver propelled **37114** and the train back two miles to Kirkton crossing, before charging back through Golspie at 40mph and finally staggering over the summit at walking pace.

By December, the leaf fall season had ended, but next came the frost and snow of a Highland winter. It wasn't that rare to get temperatures as low as -20C when working nights, and our fleet of locomotives were kept running night and day, to prevent them freezing up. Air systems would contain methylated spirit, fed via a tank on the side of the compressor, to stop brakes from freezing. Every time the AWS system went off, the cab would be filled with fumes, and a familiar smell which any down-on-his-luck tramp would instantly recognise.

1984 was one of the most memorable since I joined the industry. We had any number of firsts at our small depot, and with Chris Green now in Scotland, change was evident on an almost weekly basis. The New Year started with some fierce blizzards hitting the whole of the north of Scotland. On Thursday 12 January, **37183** had hit a fallen tree at 65mph while working the first train of the day north. The weight of ice and snow had brought the tree onto the line, and the crew of the 37 had no chance of stopping. Thankfully, despite the impact taking place at speed, the locomotive remained upright on the rails. The job was stopped for some hours, as the locomotive from the Invergordon goods was used to drag the stricken 37 with its very bent nose, and its train, back to Dingwall. I believe **37183** was sent to Swindon works for repair, and not seen again until spring.

Over the weekend of 4-5 February, further heavy snow returned with a vengeance, and at one point, all lines out of Inverness were blocked by drifting snow or fallen trees. Pat MacDonald and Donnie Sutherland got stuck in a huge drift above Achnasheen, and after spending the night aboard the 26, were airlifted out by the RAF the next day. The last train from Aberdeen was marooned in snow above Huntly, and the midday train from Wick snow-bound on the county march, with its passengers finally finding refuge in the (now closed) hotel at Forsinard. I was 2200 shed with Jock Hay, and all we saw was chaos, with the plough engines coming in from one job, being fuelled and re-manned and sent straight back out again.

In the end, the Kyle line was given the lowest priority for ploughing, Aberdeen was dealt with from the east, and the Perth plough was used on Drumochter. This left our own ploughs to deal with Aviemore, and then north to Forsinard and beyond, with a gang of hardy permanent way men, all armed with shovels to help dig out the buried train. A torrid time, but as always, the railway pulled through, although it would be over a week for any return to normal operations began. The following week, I was night shift spare, and the week was spent helping with the mopping up operations and thawing out locomotives in the wagon shops, before they could come into the shed for repair. So cold was the wind chill that the *Clansman* suffered complete freezing up of its air brakes, while waiting passage onto the single line at Dalwhinnie. The train was left to the elements once the few passengers aboard had been recovered, by bringing another train alongside.

The Class 37s seemed to be not only vulnerable to leaves but also snow and ice, with the large radiator grill being perfect for ingesting snow. Once a machine had frozen up, then some severe mechanical problems could arise, with overheating and electrical failures being the most common. It came as no surprise, as February wore on, that more and more north trains reverted to the old order, with **26037/040** working as a pair for the whole of the week commencing 12 February. Fashions come and go, but style lasts forever. Frozen locomotives were dragged onto the depot, and left in the wagon shops to thaw out by using industrial-size paraffin heaters.

On 5 March, I was rostered with Manson Milne on the 0508 freight to Elgin and Keith. When booking on, I was delighted to find that our locomotive for the day was **37114**, out on test following some heavy-duty maintenance. I was doubly delighted to find out that today, we would be running to Dufftown, to trip some whisky tanks up the valley from Keith. Of all the routes signed by Inverness men, this was the only one to have eluded me so far in my career. So, to complete the set with a lovely man like Manson, and also with one of my favourite locomotives, was, as they say, 'simply divine'.

The branch left the mainline at Keith Junction and climbed for around ten miles, up through the valley at gradients as steep as 1:60 in places. The town of Dufftown was at the heart of whisky country and had several working distilleries in the town, and also a fairly intact station and goods yard. Manson was a long-time resident of Keith, so he was very much back on home soil, as we climbed up the valley of the River Isla, past Loch Park and over the famous Glenfiddich viaduct, known to whisky drinkers the world over.

After placing our wagons in the locations needed, we shut down the engine and walked into town to one of the nicest baker's shops I've ever seen. After enjoying buttered rolls and hot tea, we rejoined the 37 as Manson kindly offered me the driver's seat for the run back to Keith, to collect the rest of our trains, and onwards to Inverness for a 1400 finish. A perfect day, and one that it was hard to believe I actually got paid for, doing something so enjoyable. A second trip up the branch followed two days later, this time with **47546**, to collect the now full wagons and take them to Keith for onwards tripping to Aberdeen by **40143**, crewed by a set of Ferryhill men.

On 26 March I was rostered with Davie Fraser on the midday passenger to Perth and back with the *Clansman*. I was thrilled to find our locomotive for the outwards trip was none other than **47525**, known to many enthusiasts as 'super duff', on account of its high-speed exploits on the ECML, back in the day. It did a competent job of getting us to Perth, although in my view, it was no better than a number of its classmates. Perhaps it was due a classified overhaul, and some of the edge taken off the machine after years of hard work. After a walk round the links, and a fish and chip tea, we returned home on 1S59, with our own 'super duff' Inverness-based **47469**, passing **40122** in Perth yard as it waited to head south with a short freight.

On 4 April, **37017** caught fire at Ardgay while heading for Wick. The local fire brigade were sent for, to dampen down the work already done by the crew with the locomotive's fire suppression system. In my experience, fires on this class of locomotive were extremely rare, and this one was caused by electrical problems. This phenomenon went on to dog **37017** for the remainder of the year, with frequent power failures and repair bookings for low amps. One driver booked the loco for loss of power, along with having a rant about the continuing problems the loco was suffering. The witty reply from fitting staff was, "if careless drivers keep losing their amps, then perhaps they should learn to take better care of them".

A YOUNG EDDIE WALLACE AND JOE POLSON (DRIVING) BACK 26041 UP ONTO THE LAST WICK IN LATE 1979.

THAT MAN POLSON AGAIN. THIS TIME TAKING THE MUIR OF ORD TO DINGWALL TOKEN ON BOARD. HARRY ARCHIBALD.

BALLYMOSS AND SEMAPHORE SIGNALLING GALORE AT ABERDEEN IN AN UNDATED SHOT

49

THE GOVERNOR OVERRIDE LEVER WHICH I PULLED FOR ALL MY WORTH ON 26011.

A YOUNGER ME AT THE CONTROLS OF 27005 ON AN ABERDEEN JOB IN 1981.

The first couple of weeks in April found me working solid, far north turns. The first week was on early shifts with a 0515 book on duty, and the second on late shift, working 1555-2225, with a mad dash to the club for last orders on Friday night. By Good Friday, after two weeks of nothing but 37s, my ears were ringing and my back aching. These locomotives, reliable as they were, would never fall into the creature comfort and crew-friendly category. The Easter weekend brought the first of the year's special trains to the Highlands, and in 1984 we saw the *Easter Highlander* arriving behind **26008/021**, to be replaced by **26035/040** for the return leg. The following Saturday saw 1Z72 arrive behind **40181**, to be replaced by **37114/183** for a trip to Kyle of Lochalsh. We passed the special at the now closed Lentran loop, as we came back from the north with **37017**, on its last run with its familiar white stripe. The following weekend, we welcomed the veteran EE Class 40 number **40015** to the Highlands, on the 1355 from Aberdeen. The machine remaining on Inverness to Aberdeen jobs until at least 8 May. Peter Mackenzie and I headed for Aberdeen with **37183** on the 1740 ex Inverness, and we passed the larger EE machine at Nairn, heading the Inverness boys, who had earlier worked to Aberdeen, back to base. Peter was a fearless driver, and we whipped the 37 up to some very high speeds on the return, to help make up some of the time lost waiting for connections of late-running south services at Aberdeen – ten seconds per quarter mile in places.

On Saturday 12 May, my own job that night, the 2000 as required for engineering trains, was cancelled, as no work was booked to take place. I was pleased to see that I had been marked up with driver Richard Grant to cover the return *Skirl of the Pipes* to Perth with **27054/055**. Much more fun than eight hours on ballast in the middle of nowhere. I cannot remember how we got home, but as with most of the Skirls, it was very much a 'rolling riot' on the southbound run.

With the start of the summer timetable on 14 May, the build-up to the introduction of the then novel radio signalling on the Kyle line got underway in earnest. Test car Iris made several visits to the line, and whenever I worked a Kyle job, cabs full of boffins seemed to be in attendance, with the second man often banished to the back cab with a newspaper. I recall one Friday morning on the first train west, when it was my driver who had to spend most of the trip in the rear cab, until his 'pan drop' mints had taken full. effect At least the comfort of **26032** allowed him to relax, and as for the boffins, they obviously thought I was a second man, passed to drive and welcomed, having an empty seat on the right-hand side to use. The Kyle line took on a feeling of melancholy and great sadness as the summer wore on. We were all used to change after the last few years, but this was change on a different scale, as it would involve the eradication of a way of life, in situ since the line first opened. Although everyone knew the new signalling would help secure the line's long-term future, the loss of so many signalling jobs was hard to bear. Men who had worked the line for most of their lives were about to be made redundant, and a way of life changed forever. One of my big regrets is that I didn't take a camera with me on many of my trips between 1980 and 1984, to capture the rapid changes taking place on our railway. On Friday 6 July, **37260** was named *Radio Highland* at Dingwall, as it headed west with the 1055 train to Kyle. Only ScotRail could delay a passenger train for over 20 minutes, while the locomotive was named.

On a more positive note, we had also begun to work our daily InterCity 125 High Speed Train service to/from Kings Cross from the start of the summer timetable. The first day the train ran was not without some further HST drama. The booked driver turned up to drive the train in full Highland dress, only to be threatened with being sent home by the TCS, unless he changed into his driver's uniform. At this point, the driver pointed out he would happily go home, but if he did, who would drive the train? A hasty compromise was reached. Sandy kept on his kilt for the naming ceremony for the power car **43092** *Highland Chieftain* prior to departure. Then he quickly changed into something more appropriate for the run to Perth. This is how the story went, but I was on the evening Wick job that day, so all the above was anecdotal and third-hand, later in the day. We worked both trains to/from Perth, much to the disgust of our colleagues based in Perth, who also threw their hat into the ring to drive these services. In my opinion, the only reason Inverness men prevailed was that with the set serviced overnight on our patch, we still needed to learn the traction, for shunting purposes anyway.

To see how well the new trains would work over the high mountains, and what demand existed for their all year-round use, initially only eight drivers undertook the three-week HST training programme. They were: Davie Sutherland, Sandy Sutherland (no relation), Jock Hay, John McKenzie, Robert Blaney, Peter Kiel, Peter McKenzie and Kenny Campbell. Both HST jobs at the depot had both a driver and second man as, in theory at least, the non-HST leg could require the use of steam heating. All the drivers would let you have a drive of their new charge, with the exception of Davie Sutherland. Big Davie was adamant that no second man would ever drive on his shift, and if one of us happened to be driving an HST service, we would often blow the horn and wave, as we passed his house in Aviemore. If he was in the garden or at the window, he would visibly shake with rage at the sight of a wee 'young boy' at the controls of such a prestigious service. Eventually, the novelty wore off, and even he was more than happy to share the driving with any of us with an ounce of ability. As time wore on, more and more drivers became trained on HSTs, without having the need to lodge away in Edinburgh or Newcastle to do so.

Another notable first that summer was a Sunday service on the Kyle line. The west coast was a hot-bed of free Presbyterian religion, and when **37183** arrived in Kyle on Sunday 29 July, it was to howls of protest by the original Men in Black, along with all manner of threats of damnation to both the crew and the bewildered passengers. Thankfully, the world didn't end, and we went back the following Sunday with **37025**. However, it really was a big deal, and a huge step forwards in opening up this part of the world to those who had reason to travel, for either commuting or pleasure. We were trail blazers, in serge uniforms, Doctor Martin boots, and armed with 105-ton locomotives and stock, even if to some, we were doing the devil's work for him, and us on time and three quarters, too! The Kyle line Sunday service was well used, and easily demonstrated the need for such trains. Over the next few years, the services north of Inverness on Sundays grew in popularity, and more frequent and longer trains were added to the timetable. It's nice to think we played a small part in breaking the mould of no trains on the Sabbath, and opening up the west coast to locals and visitors alike.

We were all saddened by the devastating events on 30 July, when the 1730 Edinburgh to Glasgow push/pull service hit a cow on the line near Polmont. The train, which was travelling at over 80mph, was immediately derailed upon impact, and sadly 13 people lost their lives. I was 1400 shed on the day of the incident, and all those of us on duty that evening felt numbed by the events as they began to unfold. We all realised the driver involved would have had little or no time to react as the tragedy unfolded before him. The incident wasn't on our patch, but we all felt its impact, and our mood was sombre for a fair few days.

THE FINEST OF THE INVERNESS EIGHT. 37183 STEAMING NICELY. COPYRIGHT DAVID SINGLETON.

A ROAMING 26038 IS SEEN AT CARLISLE WITH A VAN TRAIN ON 14/6/83.

I spent my two-week summer holidays in the fleshpots of San Antonio, on a Club 18-30 in Ibiza, and returned to work on 17 September with an ungodly 0330 alarm call. My first turn of duty was to be a trip to Aberdeen on the 0600 departure, returning home with the 0945 service, arrival time in Inverness at 1205. With a holiday to get out of my system, I recall being back home in bed by 1400 for another solid few hours' sleep. In fact, with another 0330 alarm call the next day, I suspect I only got out of my bed for a meal at around 1900. With a rest day on Wednesday, I would have been back to normal afterwards, and ready for a trip on the far north with **37011** on the Saturday. This interloper was sent up to bolster the ranks of the Inverness 8, which at the time were having an appalling dip in form, with some days only two locomotives available for traffic.

With the miners' strike still raging, a desperate government looked at new ways to get coal into the UK, ahead of the long winter months, and the real possibility of a humiliating defeat for Thatcher. Somebody, somewhere, came up with the plan to ship coal into the country from overseas, through the deep-water harbour at Invergordon. Out of sight and out of mind, I suppose. The heavily unionised rail industry was never going to move the coal, so the job was given to road haulage instead.

On Thursday 11 October, the late Duncan Finlayson and I had a Class 47 on the 1220 to Glasgow. We left Pitlochry on time at 1415, with me in the driving seat. As we ran alongside the A9 at Ballinluig, a convoy of coal-carrying lorries (from a well-known Lanarkshire strike breaker) was quickly overtaken, as they all headed for Ravenscraig steelworks. Duncan, being a staunch union man, ran to the cab door and opened it, before making some hugely rude gestures to each of the truck drivers as we passed by. Unfortunately, as we approached Dunkeld, the distant was on and we were brought to a stand in the loop, to await the arrival of a late-running northbound service. We must have waited slightly longer than usual, as one by one, the trucks we had passed earlier, began to stop outside of the station. Soon, several very big and angry looking drivers began to head our way. I alerted Duncan to incoming hostiles on the platform, who by now, was looking like he may be regretting his earlier actions. Thankfully, at that very moment we got the right away, and Duncan, despite me being in the driving seat, pulled the power handle right to notch 8, as we rocketed out of the station, and more importantly the danger zone. Duncan definitely kept his head down on arrival in Perth, and declined a walk into town with the guard and me, despite it being a lovely autumn afternoon.

The onset of autumn brought the usual mayhem with train running on the Wick line. The old order returned with 26/37 combinations proving to be the preferred method of operation. However, as the Class 26 overhaul programme was gathering pace, the number of steam heat-fitted machines dwindled, causing headaches for the operating department. Although the class had worked the routes before on a sporadic basis, Class 27s began to appear in ever-increasing numbers, even managing to work Kyle trains solo. As a consequence, the drivers at Wick and Thurso had to be given a day's training course on the slightly more powerful locomotives. Ironically, however, the Class 27s also figured in the region's early withdrawal plan.

On 24 October, I was rostered with Davie Sutherland and Willie Flood to run light engine to Invergordon to collect some whisky tanks from the distillery, just north of the station. This was all that remained of the fan of sidings which used to serve two distilleries, the Invergordon smelter and also the North Sea pipe fabrication yard of MK Shands. As we creaked into the yard with **37262** over the rusty rails, it was plain to see that nothing much had passed this way for some time. With only four tanks to collect, we were back in Inverness in no time at all. I have never set foot in the place since.

On Monday 29 October, I received the good news that my time had come to return to Edinburgh in early 1985, to undertake my MP12 driver training. Without sounding big-headed, it was something of a formality, as it was for most of my colleagues as well. That's not to say we didn't have lots to learn —

of course we did, especially on the rules and regulations side of the job. However, after serving a five-year apprenticeship with some of the best drivers in the country, the technical skills were firmly embedded. However, before then, we still had a winter to get through, and with the weather turning cold, and our fragile motive power showing no signs of improvement, thoughts of warm classrooms and endless nights in bed had to be put to the back of my mind.

In late October, **37264** came to Inverness to help build some resilience into our crumbling fleet. My first encounter with it was on 24 November, when Davie Fraser and I brought it back from Brora, on the midday train from Wick. I must say that I went on to find 264 to be an excellent machine and a welcome addition to our ranks. In its early days at Inverness, it was easily recognisable, as it was the only one not to carry miniature snow ploughs. In the week leading up to Christmas, my rostered job all week was *The Royal Highlander* to Perth and home, with the combined Glasgow/Edinburgh internal arriving in Inverness at 0440. I loved being on these jobs at this time of year. The London sleeping car trains were always packed with people going away for the holidays, and on the return service the train would carry anything up to seven vans, all jammed full of letters and parcels as part of the last-minute Christmas rush. The train was booked to dwell at both Kingussie and Aviemore for over ten minutes, as much of the train's contents would be off-loaded for various destinations on Speyside. With cold, crisp, starry nights, warm cabs and good company, it was a pleasure to be at work. Traction-wise we had nothing special, and **47546** and **47522** both worked on more than one occasion. However, with a new girlfriend to keep entertained and happy, I took the unusual step of taking the whole of Christmas off on annual leave. My last turn of duty for 1984 was on Saturday 22 December. So, another eventful year ended on a whimper. With more traffic lost, an expansion of single manning, the never-ending miners' strike, and the closure of manual signal boxes on the Kyle road, it was a bleak midwinter. Sadly, we had not yet reached the end, and 1985 would prove to be an even more eventful year in our contracting little world.

TIMELESS. LOCO, HOTEL, GOOD SHED AND SIGNALS. ALL NOW LONG GONE. COPYRIGHT HARRY ARCHIBALD.

A FINE SELECTION OF SEMAPHORES WITH THE DEPOT BEHIND. COPYRIGHT HARRY ARCHIBALD.

26044 AND THE 1115 TO WICK ON 26/5/79, THE FORMER FOUNDRY CHIMNEY IS BEHIND AND THE BRSA STAFF CLUB ON EXTREME RIGHT.

Chapter 4 - Passed For Driving

1985 started pretty much in the same vein as the old year had ended, with a biting east wind and hard overnight frosts. My first trip of the year involved a spin to Aberdeen and back with **47274**, with a couple of days on the HST turn to Perth completing week one. On the Friday, we whipped **43091** and its mate **43042** up to 108mph in a vain attempt to make up lost time, following a bad crossing with *The Royal Highlander*. It was the fastest speed I have ever witnessed on our patch, then and since.

On 11 January, the air system on **37264** froze up, rendering us a complete failure at Tain, as we returned from Brora, with temperatures deep into double digits. **37262** came to our rescue after an hour's delay, so not bad, all things considered. The following Sunday, we had the same problem with **37048**, this time on an engineer's train, once again at Tain. The compressor governor froze solid and prevented power from being taken. It was no time to be dropping rails anyway, as the mercury hit minus 17 over much of the Highlands that night. On 21 January, **47102** had a frozen boiler and cracked water tubes at Aberdeen, so we had to swop locomotives at Ferryhill, and come home with **47405** instead, as the prospect of 108 miles with no heat just wasn't on the agenda. On 26 January, the same happened with **47211**, but this time, **27005/27048** was the more than able replacement. The boiler smith's workload was always high as temperatures dropped.

After weeks of biting cold, snow hit the Highlands big time, late in the month, and by Monday 27th the area was in chaos. That day, I booked on with Dan MacLennan (no relation) for the 1735 to Wick. The first locomotive we prepared was **27005**, which we found to have no working boiler, due to snow and ice freezing the water tank. We finally left 90 minutes late, with **26040** and **27055** in multiple – a rare combination for the north lines. The southbound train was also having a torrid time. **37114** had been taken off the branch, due to **27014** struggling alone, after its paired mate **27048** had failed completely. When we boarded the footplate at Rogart in white-out conditions, we found none of the locomotives had a working boiler, and the few passengers aboard were in abject misery. It was a cold and silent trip home, as once again, we had let our passengers down. The snow and ice lasted most of the following week, and despite, no doubt having problems of their own, Eastfield sent **37175** to help keep some semblance of service going on the north line. Some days we did, and sometimes we didn't, but all I can report all these years later is, it wasn't for the want of trying, as everyone went the extra mile to do all they could to keep wheels turning. Thursday 7 February was my last shift before heading for Edinburgh and six months of training undertaking MP12. My driver for the day, Jack Fraser, wished me all the best as we cruised back from Brora on the midday train, on the very excellent and very strong **37175**.

As the driver training course had more in-depth content than MP11, we travelled down on Sunday evening, ready for a 9am start on the Monday. This gave a useful additional seven hours' pay, along with the industry-accepted principle of those undertaking training to be paid an average of the previous two months' earnings. This arrangement was known as L215, which was the number of the nationally agreed minute covering average earnings. In my case, this equated to a 44-hour week, plus the travelling payment, so all in all, this was a nice little earner, with 51 hours' pay every week as a minimum. The MP12 training course involved five weeks of rules and regulations training, and nine weeks of traction training, followed by a further ten weeks back at home depot, putting it all into practice, and brushing up on our already well-honed driving skills. My fellow trainees were Peter Carmody from Inverness, Graham Johnson from Aberdeen, Jim and John from Perth, Alan Gilzean and his pal from Haymarket, and last but not least, a chap from Fort William, making up the maximum classroom ration of eight men to a single instructor. Out in the yard or on the operational railway, it was a maximum of 1:4.

After a five-year gap, it was back to the Lairg hotel. With other Inverness drivers down learning the HST, we were never short of good company. With no Deltics to occupy my time, the week was usually made up of a couple of nights with John Thain on the West Highland Line on the 1650 out to Bridge of Orchy, or to Dundee and back with the 1638 ex Glasgow QS. Either of the above trains was more often than not driven by the legendary Peter Walker of Eastfield. Then we'd have a couple of nights swimming up in the Commonwealth pool, and last but not least, a Thursday night on the town. With only a half-day in class on Friday, any hangover could just about be suffered, even if breakfast had been missed.

Only as the course progressed did I fully realise how little we, on the right-hand side of the cab, really knew, in relation to the man on the left. Our rules knowledge was at best rudimentary, and it was only when Dick Forrest worked through the rules/regulations in detail that my attainment levels matured. It was the same with traction. Yes, I could drive. But fault finding and undertaking thorough preparation prior to service showed me up for the complete novice that I was.

The Scottish region was well into a policy of standardising its locomotive deployment. The Class 47 and Class 37 were used as the region's passenger engines, and Class 20 or 27 and anything available used for freight. So, we learned both the 47 and 27 at Haymarket, and undertook conversion training onto other types later on, back at home depot.

After a riotous three months in Edinburgh, with every weekend off duty, it was back to Inverness to complete my training, and back to the real world. On Friday 2 August, after a three-day passing out parade, culminating in driving **37025** to Dingwall and returning with **47157** on the Invergordon commuter service, Inspector Bruce told me that I was now passed for driving. He said that after signing all the necessary paperwork, we should adjourn to the railway club to celebrate with drinks. I am glad he said "we", as I finally rolled out of the club some ten hours later, well and truly gassed, and in need of my bed. By nightfall, I had lost my hat, my dignity and, once safely home, the contents of my stomach.

On Sunday 4th, it was back to shift work and down to earth with a bump, as a week of nights beckoned. We worked the up *Royal Highlander* to Perth and back with the internal overnight. My first legal drive was with **47441**.Over the course of the week, we had **47517/47604/47578/47532** and **47614**, and every train on time.

Week commencing August 21st was my first full week on the recently-introduced commuter train from Invergordon. We booked on at 0510, and went empty coaches (ECS) to Invergordon, before forming the 0710 all stations back to Inverness. The locomotive and stock came off an Aberdeen diagram, so a solid Class 47. We had **47117/47210/47009/210** and **47269** on the Friday, which made a nice change from the norm. I guess that fledging commuter train was the start of what is now a fairly comprehensive 'Invernet' commuter market.

Jock Russell and I had a novel day out on Sunday 22 September. We took **43061/154** to Aberdeen at 1005 on the diverted Inverness to Kings Cross service, calling at all principal stations. This gave the likes of Forres its first direct London service since the closure of the Dava route. At Aberdeen, we gave our HST to a Ferryhill man, for the next leg to Edinburgh. On the return, another Mark 3 set was bagged this time, with **47711** leading on a diverted Edinburgh to Inverness train formed of a spare Edinburgh to Glasgow rake. It was a wonderful late summer's day, and Jock was his usual exuberant self. It was one of those shifts that passed very quickly. No coupling on/off or a boiler to operate - a great day for posing! A week later, we went from shining HSTs to BRCW Type 2, when we had **26024/026** on my last ever passenger trip over the Highland Line.

On 30 September, I obtained my first driving turn. Denny Ross and I had taken **37021** to Brora on the last train north. Our return working had **37260/261** in tandem, and therefore needed two drivers. Denny, to his credit, put me on the front locomotive, and he went on 261. So, as I headed off into the night with **Radio Highland**, my driving career had begun in earnest. Back then, a passed man was paid driver's rate for the whole shift, irrespective of how many hours of actual driving they had performed, so a nice little earner, as the saying goes.

A few days later, my world came crashing down when, at the controls of **37183** on the same train, we collided with the level crossing gates at Lairg. They had remained closed, due to engineering works in connection with the fitment of RETB to the north lines. Thankfully, nothing was hurt except my pride, but it was a salutatory lesson on how quickly things can go wrong. I felt terrible for days afterwards and kept playing the whole scenario over and over in my mind. In fact, for years afterwards, I had dreams of the sickening crunch as the 37 demolished the flimsy wooden gates in a matter of seconds. At least I saved the PW boys all the hassle of spending a night removing them.

On Wednesday 9 October, I witnessed the locomotive ex 1S25 arriving on the fuel bay, with its Number 2 end bogie on fire. I used every available fire extinguisher I could find to quench the flames licking from below **47535**, and felt my firefighting skills had offset some of the damage caused to the level crossing the previous week. Sadly, my Train Crew Manager did not see it that way, and a few days later, I received a disciplinary charge for damaging the board's property. Ironically, I didn't even get a thank-you for saving another piece of the board's property in **47535**. Life's a bitch, as they say.

On 18 November, they finally got around to my disciplinary hearing for the Lairg incident. Despite the best efforts of my spokesman, I was banged to rights and had a reprimand placed on my file, which to my knowledge, is there to this day. I did have one stroke of luck, though. After my hearing, I had to go with Davie Irvine and **47003** to Aberdeen, as somebody had gone sick. With two hours 20 minutes mileage payment, I was ribbed for weeks afterwards that I was the first person ever to make money from crime.

On Sunday 24 November, we had a repeat of the earlier HST run to Aberdeen. This time, we had **43042/157,** and home with **47708**. The 47 was in a real mess, no doubt after years of abuse on the E&G services. We struggled for amps. The engine room was awash with oil, and the cab cold and very draughty, so no posing today. We lost time on just about every section. My driver, mild-mannered Jock McKenzie, was totally wound up, and failed the 47/7 upon arrival in Inverness. With so many faults to report, he filled two pages on the locomotive's repair book.

On 27 November, I had another go at laying detonators, after **47540** suffered a main generator flashover between Moy and Tomatin on the midday Glasgow train. **47467** came to our rescue after a reasonable 45-minute delay. We had **Bill Burrell** every evening that week on the down *Clansman*, **47562** putting in a solid performance.

I secured my second driving turn on 12 December, when Willie Butler put me on **37261** as the train engine on the 1205 from Wick. Willie himself took charge of the leading locomotive **37114**.

On Sunday 15 December, RETB was finally commissioned on the Wick line. My first trip was on 18 December, when Raymond Mackay and I went to Brora and back with **37261** and **37264**. We ran on time both ways, which came as a surprise, as the system was proving to be unreliable, and many attempts were needed at certain stations, such as Ardgay, to obtain a token. Or, in extreme circumstances, the driver would need to go to the back cab, to use the working radio there at every station. I guess we must have been lucky, as it took well into 1986 for things to settle down. I believe at one point, serious consideration was being given to a return to electric token working, although without any operational semaphores. The Wick boys used to tell us they would hear the skippers of trawlers holding conversations with each other on the alleged secure RETB channel, as our men tried to enter the system on the first train of the day south. I have no idea what the Derby boffins would have made of that, as they were long gone by now, no doubt spending their Christmas bonus for a job well done.

Another notable event took place on Saturday 21 December. Raymond and I were 1400 shed, when we received a call from the TCS Jock Robertson, to tell us **37262** was in trouble on the midday train from Wick. We were to take **37417** (the 37/4 training locomotive) and run as 1Z99 to assist. Fortunately, Raymond was passed to drive the new traction, and I was thrilled to enjoy an afternoon out on such a clean and shiny locomotive. We caught up with **37262** at Tain and hauled it and its train back to Inverness. To the best of my knowledge, this was the first ever passenger working of a Class 37/4 north of Inverness. As Max Boyce would have sung, "I was there", as were Bob Barlow, and many others.

I used up my accrued leave from my MP12 course, and enjoyed another Christmas away from work, albeit with a different girlfriend than the previous year. I returned on Saturday 28 December, as fierce blizzards hit the area. Walking through the station to sign on duty in driving snow, I was not optimistic for a normal day. The London sleeper 1S25 finally arrived in town, a little over three hours late, as Drumochter was whited out, and the A9 long since closed. Due to no available RETB-fitted 37s, we did not depart with the 1135 to Wick until almost 1230. This was after once **37114** was given a quick turnaround, after arriving itself an hour late, with the first train from the north. Despite our late running, we still ran all the way to Helmsdale, as the midday train from Wick was itself nearly two hours late, due to the usual carnage taking place up in the Sutherland hills. I remember crunching through knee deep snow, as we walked round to climb in the warm cab of **37261** for the run home. With more snow and frozen points heading south, we finally arrived in Inverness at almost 1800. This, of course, had a knock-on effect on the last train north, as it had to wait for **37261** to be serviced before it could depart, at well after 1900. No wooden dollar performance regimes back then, thank goodness! Just a collective desire to do the best we could and keep the railway open when roads were shut. Now, though, it often seems the other way round.

The New Year brought the usual weather-related problems, along with a new set of challenges. This was the first year that I remember mess room talk of the possible replacement of locomotive-hauled services with multiple units, and the whole of the Inverness area becoming a DMU-only railway. As if this wasn't bad enough, we also saw further erosion of the role of the driver's assistant. Most of our time was spent around the station and depot or on local freight workings, as all our Perth jobs, other than at night, were now single manned. With the imminent introduction of ETH on nearly all the remaining steam heat services, the future looked grim. Little did I know, as I booked on duty for 1400 shed on the second day of the year, that this would be my last full year based at the depot. Davie Irvine and I had a really busy day as locomotives were woken up and serviced, after the holiday layover. Adam Sutherland, the TCS, appreciated our hard work. He allowed us to finish duty at 2000, as we had a few men booking on spare, due to no freight services running that night. Davie caught the 2030 home to Aviemore, as I adjourned to the railway club with hard-as-nails Ronnie Donaldson for a few pints, with both of us in a reflective and sombre mood.

The following week, Ronnie and I were rostered together on a week of Aberdeen jobs. It was almost a steam heat full house, as we enjoyed trips with **47009/47157/47209/47517** and **37263**, as a late replacement for failed **47562**. It was an excellent week, and Ronnie was an excellent mate to spend time with. His nickname was 'The Beat', as he was the self-appointed depot hard man. We often took the rise out of him, with various renditions of the pop song *I am the Beat,* sung by The Look. He used to feign anger, as a boy band of second men sang, "all over the world people know my name, I'm in demand, and I am the beat". He used to respond by holding up his massive left fist, and tell us it was a night in hospital, and his right fist, a week.

RICHARD GRANT TAKES **37025** TO THE DEPOT OFF THE FIRST ONE IN FROM WICK ON **13/5/85.**

37414 AND THE ROYAL SCOTSMAN AT KEITH IN **1985.**

BOBBY HOBAN BACKS **40170** ON TO A SUNDAY DEPARTURE FOR THE SOUTH. COPYRIGHT RAIL-ONLINE.CO.UK

WITH THE FIRST OF THE BIG CLIMBS OVER A **40** ARRIVES AT KINGUSSIE WITH THE **1240** EX INVERNESS. COPYRIGHT RAIL-ONLINE.CO.UK

JACK FRASER BACKS HIS **25** ONTO A FAILED **47** FOR THE RUN TO INVERNESS AT AVIEMORE IN **1977**. COPYRIGHT RAIL-ONLINE.CO.UK

A REGULAR OCCURRENCE AS AN ADDITIONAL LOCO IS WORKED NORTH TO BALANCE THE ETH REQUIREMENTS AT INVERNESS. COPYRIGHT HARRY ARCHIBALD.

DIGGING 26021 OUT OF A BIG DRIFT UP ON THE LUIB WINTER 1984. COPYRIGHT DAVE DUNCAN

THERE IS NOTHING SO GRAND IN THE WHOLE OF THE LAND AS TO BE AT THE DANCING IN KYLE. **26032** RUNS ROUND AFTER ARRIVING WITH AN INSPECTION SALOON. COPYRIGHT HARRY ARCHIBALD.

47704 AFTER ARRIVAL IN PERTH WITH THE CLANSMAN. THIS WAS JUST PRIOR TO THE PUSH/PULL ERA WHEN THE LOCOMOTIVES ROAMED FAR AND WIDE.

THE DAILY HST SERVICE TO LONDON IS SEEN IN PLATFORM 2 NOT LONG AFTER ITS INAUGURATION IN MAY 1984. COPYRIGHT HARRY ARCHIBALD.

37102 OF MARCH DEPOT IS SEEN AT THURSO ON 12/6/84. THIS WAS AT THE HEIGHT OF THE TYPE 3 SHORTAGES IN INVERNESS WITH LOCOMOTIVES BEING DRAFTED IN FROM FAR AND WIDE.

On Tuesday 14 January, a shining ex works **37418** set sail for Kyle on the 0655 service. Sadly, it got no further than Garve, as the locomotive hit a tree near Fodderty, causing a fair amount of damage to the front end of 418. We happened to be at Garve with **37025** on a ballast drop, so at least a rescue locomotive was at hand. After the usual quick exchange, we limped back home with a poorly ETH machine. **37025**, with its boiler simmering nicely, was worked hard to make up lost time for the west. I took a few days off at the end of the week, to enjoy some last steam heat 37s of my own to Wick/Thurso. From 20 January, every train was booked, in theory at least, for ETH. After a successful few days of chasing steam heat 37s and drinking copious amounts of night-time beer in The Phoenix with like-minded friends who would all then crash in my town centre flat. My first turn back was on the nightshift on 20 January, when **37183** left Inverness for the last time, as pilot to **47541** on the internal overnight. I'm not sure if it ever came back to visit us again. I spent the whole of the week on nights with Pat MacDonald. From Tuesday onwards, it snowed and snowed, and as usual we kept going, although the timetable fell apart. We arrived back in Inverness late every morning with the *Royal Highlander*. The lateness varied between 45 minutes and 180 minutes. We both loved our overtime, so it wasn't a huge problem, although a dose of the 'nodding dogs' was hard to keep at bay, especially when in the driving seat. However, lady luck smiled on me, as the only morning we ran to time was on the Saturday, when **47578** got us in bang on 0800. This allowed a few hours' sleep, before getting the weekend underway with a lunch-time game of snooker in the 147 club on Union Street, followed by an afternoon in various bars, before finally dancing the night away in Dillinger's night club. The night rate, overtime and mileage payments earned during the week all help fund a grand night, along with a weapons-grade hangover. Work hard, play hard – and why not, at 23 years of age?

A tottering plastic nightmare arrived in town at the end of the month. **150001** was allocated to the 1115 Wick service from 27 January onwards, with the trip booked to be single manned, doubtless as a new model management statement of the future for us all. My role was therefore to travel passenger to Brora on this hideous contraption, before working the more conventional 37/4 home. The sprinter was struggling big-time with the arduous task of running trains over this totally underrated route. The look on passengers' faces was priceless, as this baby 3 car train replaced their more usual five-coach rake. No buffet, nowhere for mail and no portion for Thurso, but cheap as chips to operate, which I remain pretty sure was all that really mattered. By Wednesday, the thing was wheezing along on two engines and dropping time on every section. By Friday, we were all royally sick to death of it. If this was the future, then God help us all. I was more than delighted to climb into the cabs of **37415/37417** and **37420**, for a return to normality. I had seen the future, and it wasn't one I was keen to be part of.

In the week commencing 10 February, it was my turn to learn our new ETH 37s. Our instructor, Jock Hay, gave us a thorough talk on the differences from a conventional 37, along with a look round **37414**, to help us identify the new locations of isolating cocks, governors, fuses and the all-important new electronics, in the former boiler compartment. On Thursday, we got to drive **37417** and **37418** on north jobs, before the all-important pass out with Inspector Bruce on Friday. Job done, more beers in celebration, felt like the order of the day, so it was off to the nearest bar for a few scoops with another locomotive on my ever-growing traction card.

Saturday 22 February is another day that will be remembered for a very long time. Jock Russell and I were rostered to work Saturday night on ballast on a track re-laying job between Kingussie and Newtonmore. The Highlands were in the middle of another bitterly cold spell. Temperatures had remained at or below zero for at least a week. Our locomotive for the night was Motherwell's **37125**, a real bag of nails, both inside and out. We left Inverness under a clear sky, with almost 700 tons of rails and another crew on

37261 pushing us from behind for all they were worth. As we climbed away from sea level, the cab cooled down rapidly, and brass monkeys were expected to appear from the nose end at any moment. We passed the last passenger train at Aviemore, and set off along the Spey valley, with a horror film-style mist rising off the river. By the time we arrived at the worksite, I felt colder than I had done for many years, and still with the prospect of six hours work ahead of us. To cut a long story short, by 2am, the temperature outside was almost minus 25 degrees. It was so cold that we had to climb into the brake van and huddle round the roaring stove, in a vain attempt to keep warm. Before long, we had the whole of the permanent way squad in with us. With us all in misery and no chance of doing much work, after off-loading the rails, the ganger cancelled further work, and sensibly chased us all off-site and home. I was still frozen to the bone, as I climbed into bed two hours later. This side of the job was never seen by the public or management. It certainly justified every penny of the night and weekend enhanced pay we received for these unsocial duties.

Such was the reduction in workload at the depot for double-manned turns that my next trip out on the road wasn't until 6 March. ETH 47s both ways on freight jobs further showed the spare capacity the region now had. **47425** to Perth for **47632** home made for a maximum mileage freight trip. The following week, **47155** found no better employment than on ballast drops between Muir of Ord and Dingwall. With RETB restricted to north and west of here, at least some variety still existed along the shores of the Beauly Firth. Passenger-wise, the north and west was solid 37/4, Aberdeen 47/0 and the Perth road ETH 47, with just about every turn single-manned. On 14 April, we had **47214** steaming on the 1750 ex Aberdeen, after our original locomotive **47635** was commandeered for something needier out of the Granite City. Ironically, the next day, the situation was reversed. On arrival in Aberdeen, our locomotive **47461** and stock were used to form 1505 Aberdeen to Glasgow, to cover for a failure. As a consequence, our lucky passengers on the 1750 to Inverness enjoyed Mark 2 air-conditioned comfort, hauled by **47476** off the earlier failure. The week ended with more ETH freight, when we took **47614** to Muir of Ord to collect some grain hoppers.

In the week commencing 21 April, I was delighted to find that I had been selected for a couple of weeks' training on Class 08 shunting locomotives. The endless days of spare turns had no appeal for me, and I would always rather be out on the road doing something or other. I loved these strong little engines, or 'pilots', as we knew them. Later, at Ayr, they were called 'puggies'. We had two very productive weeks with Rory MacDonald, mostly spent driving **08717** in and around the station, followed by the end-of-course Inspector Bruce pass out, and beers on Platform 8.

As spring turned to summer, more work was lost, and even some of the freight traffic went single-manned as well. The guards thought that it was all good sport, and our loss would be their gain. In their minds, our eradication would save them, and in future, all trains would only carry a driver and guard. How wrong they were! After the BRB had killed off the role of driver's assistant, the roll-out of full Driver Only Operation (DOO) began. It definitely felt like a long game had been played, following our resistance in 1982. Revenge is indeed best served cold. Within the next few years, the role of goods guard was also eliminated, to be replaced by the ubiquitous Train (WO) man concept in 1988. This would end forever the clear demarcation line of promotion from the back of the train to the front not being allowed.

Things had got so bad that I had to take a second job, like many rail staff of the time. In my case, it was a role as a barman in the Coach House Inn, just outside town. My normal shifts would be 1700/2000 on Sundays, the same single mid-week night on a revolving basis, and also 1700/2300 on Friday. If the adjacent Annabel's night club was short-staffed, then my Friday night shift would be extended until 0300

Saturday morning. On more than one occasion, I left the night club at 0300, went home via a furious pedal on my bike for a shower, and booked on duty for the 0355 Aberdeen or 0400 prep. Sleep could wait until after work.

On other occasions, I left work with a young lady, went back to my flat, and enjoyed her company, before heading straight to work for a lunchtime book on. We could do those things when young. As the wonderfully evocative song by Alphaville goes, "I want to be forever young".

16 May was a bad day – a black Friday, in fact. Eddie Gunn and I were rostered to book on at 0618 for the 0718 oil tanks to Lairg. North of Dingwall, so "can we have an RETB-fitted locomotive, please?" "Try **37262**," said our foreman. We did, but it wouldn't start. "**37261** next," said Jock. "The brake blocks are paper-thin, so no good for traffic," replied Eddie. It was third time lucky, with **37114** doing the job, albeit with late running.

The following day, we had another trip with **37114**, this time to Kyle of Lochalsh on the prestigious *Royal Scotsman*. This was a summer-only job, obviously, and involved us going passenger to Keith, bringing the train off the Dufftown branch, and then off to Kyle via the Rose St curve. Normally, this was a through engine, but on this occasion the filthy-rich passengers enjoyed an engine change, as **37014** had to be replaced by **37114** for the run west. **37014** was banger blue, filthy inside and out, and it was a pleasure to get off the ED nag for one of our own. I've no idea what Americans paying the money to use the train, thought of it all! Not much, given the hedonistic behaviour going on inside the train at times, from what we were told by the hospitality staff we sometimes met at the end of our shift.

When the summer timetable began at the end of May, there were further changes to our work schedules. The Invergordon goods went over to being single-manned as PNB facilities were available at the midpoint in the diagram, for the driver to have his food break. This wasn't the case if it was running north of Tain, in which case conventional manning arrangements still prevailed. The remaining freight trains around Inverness were covered by a 1024 to 1824 tripper. This could cover Elgin, Burghead, Muir of Ord or Culloden Moor. My first go at the tripper was with Davie Irvine, and we managed to derail **37262** in the yard at Burghead. I was meant to be going to the cinema that night with my girlfriend, Yvonne, to see *9½ Weeks*. Sadly, due to a set of defective points, I never made it, and neither did we. Our relationship ended as few weeks later, after I couldn't attend a family party due to the inconvenient fact that I was rostered on the *Royal Scotsman* with our very own **37114**, and driver John Low The following day, we had another 'best bib and tucker' day, pass to Elgin and then work the *Northern Belle* to Kyle, with an engine change on the Rose Street curve. This time we had **47637** off and **37262** on for the RETB section. We passed **37114** and the *Scotsman* somewhere along the way, although my notes and memory fail me as to where.

After a couple of trips under my belt to Burghead, I was then happy to sign it off as a driver. It was a good route for a driving turn. On 13 August, I took **26038** down the branch with some grain wagons for the maltings. Getting down there was one thing, but getting back out was another. With such a long section between Forres and Elgin, you could wait for hours for a slot to leave the branch and get safely to Elgin yard, out of the way. Some wag had written on the ground frame at Alves, "Mummy, has Daddy left home forever?' 'No son, he's waiting to get off the Burghead branch, that's all."

An amusing incident took place at Blair Atholl on the Friday night. I was doing the Dalwhinnie to Perth driving leg of the *Royal Highlander*. As was the custom at Blair, we stopped with the loco off the end and on the level crossing. This allowed as much of the train as possible to be on the platform for passenger and post office use. As we waited time, several people began to gather at the crossing gates, waiting to cross, presumably to access the cottages and campsite down by the riverside. After a few minutes, a very pretty and slightly drunk young lady lifted up her top to reveal a perfect pair of sun-tanned breasts. With a winning sultry smile, she said, 'would you like to come back to our tent and help my friend play with these?', as she jiggled those near perfect boobs, in case I was in any doubt as to what she meant. I looked across at my driver, and knew that if I asked, if I could get off there and be picked up on the way back, he would say, 'no chance'. So sadly, I had to decline her kind offer. As we set off towards Perth, my mind was elsewhere, wishing I had been with any one of at least half a dozen drivers who would have given me the nod to get off and be collected on the way back at around 2am. Time and a quarter for representing Scotland in a tent would have gone down very nicely, but sadly, it wasn't to be. So, it wasn't just our football team that didn't really score much in the summer of '86.

Another new summer Sunday job was with the HST to Perth and back. This wasn't unusual in itself, but we did have almost six hours to kill in the fair city. With the turn operating under special manning arrangements which could only apply on a Sunday, the diagram was in excess of eleven hours, so it had to be double-manned for safety reasons. My only trip on the turn came on 17 August, when Freddy Masson and I had **43081/102** to Perth and **43107/162** home, after a mega fester in the near-deserted city. With Sunday licencing hours, I don't think we even managed a couple of pints in the Twa Tams public house. While management very much had the upper hand with diagramming issues, to be fair, our staff representatives fought tooth and nail to ensure every job which had legitimate reasons to be double-manned indeed was, with no exception or concession.

Another driving turn came my way on 20 August. **37418** and **37262** would not work in multiple on the 1135 to Wick. Driver Jim Duncan, aka 'The Duke', as he looked like a certain Hollywood actor, put me on **37262** as the train engine, and piloted me with the 37/4. The Inverness-based 37/4s were going through a bad patch, as the next day we had **37261** on its own, as no ETH machine was available.

On 28 August, I booked on for 0500 spare, to immediately be told that I was driving for the day. I needed to prepare **47297**, take Cameron McKinnon with me, and go all speed to Aviemore, as **37056** was doing all the work on the Oxwellmains to Inverness cement, after its mate **37027** had shut down. With the train regularly loading to over 1,000 tons, we needed all the amps from my 47 and the remaining healthy 37 to get over Slochd and safely into Millburn Yard. It's also worth placing on record at this point, how the Inverness-based Traincrew Supervisors (TCS) did all they could to get us under-utilised young men driving turns. While they would never sell management short, they looked after the men. I will always be grateful and remember them fondly for their actions at this difficult time, with earnings cut, and mortgages and bills to be paid.

On 13 September, I was rostered driver for a Scottish Rail Preservation Society rail tour to Kyle. We took the usual 1240 departure ex Inverness charter slot, and enjoyed a superb run to Kyle and back with **37417**. We followed the 1710 from Kyle all the way home. Consequently, my second man Fraser Munro and I had time for several beers in the railway club, before going our separate ways at around 2200.

Two days later, I was once again 'Driver MacLennan', this time on another summer-only train serving the recently re-opened station at Dunrobin Castle. The station had been re-opened to allow visitors rail access to the Duke of Sutherland's impressive home by the sea. Unfortunately, it wasn't **37114** that I took to the castle of its name, but a much more mundane **37415**. The train was booked to run round at Helmsdale, so

I also gained two hours 20 minutes mileage payment too. Very nice, and with an autumn holiday to Ibiza coming up, all very welcome.

To end a rather eventful month, on 29 September, we took the last *Royal Scotsman* of the year from Boat of Garten through to Perth with **37188**, before returning home passenger, later in the afternoon. The turn involved running light up the privately-owned Spey side line to collect the train, which had spent the night at Boat of Garten. I know this job brought back happy memories for several of the ex-Aviemore drivers, as the former main line over the Dava Moor was often reminisced over, and clearly missed.

Further signs of the retrenchment of the old order came early in October. I had a whole week of Aberdeen jobs, and every train was ETH in the form of **47430/47541/47614** and **47643**. Even the drivers were new, with Ken Nichols and Vernon Grosvenor both recent incomers from down south, along with the infamous KP Lees arriving from Motherwell. The long-standing 'Inverness drivers' jobs for Inverness men' were now under threat, and by the end of the year, we would have a further two drivers from England taking jobs that at one time would have gone to our own passed men. It definitely caused some bad feeling, and for a while, anger prevailed. After a period of the incomers being treated quite badly, an uneasy truce developed, but we were entering heavily shark-infested and uncharted waters.

Any enthusiast travelling on the Euston to Inverness sleeper on 9 October enjoyed some rare Class 37 haulage, when Dave Fraser and I took **37129** to Carrbridge to help an ailing **47467** climb Slochd. The next day, we were in the same area with **37133**, although sadly no rescue jobs took place. We made do with wagons of ballast which needed moving to Inverness.

For the rest of the month, I never left the confines of the shed, although I did have a week's leave thrown in. My confinement to shed ended on 5 November, when the excellent **37414** and **37415** stormed us to Brora and back, on late evening trains. We went one better five days later, when **37262** and **37415** were had in a pair on the same train. **37421** had failed on the branch, and **37262** was utilised as its replacement. The steam heat machine must have rediscovered its liking for passenger work, as on 19 November, we had it along with **37421** (on test) on the 0655 to Kyle.

On 26 November, Frankie Boyd and I had **37261** and **37418** on the first train north, after **37415** had thrown in the towel on the branch. The Thurso boys seemed hard task masters with the locos they had on the short six-mile branch line, as at least once per week, a broken one was returned to Inverness for some TLC.

On Tuesday 9 December, I had my eleventh and final driving turn for the year. It was only on the 0600 shed turn. However, they were all welcome from a monetary perspective, also because once a passed driver had been credited with 100 driving turns, then a very welcome pay increment could be claimed. It was only a few pounds per week more on basic pay, but every little helps, so to speak. It meant that all future aggregated wages would be at the higher rate. So, as 1986 drew to a close, it was eleven down and 89 to go. The week leading up to Christmas was once again spent on the Perth road, and trips with the internal overnight and down *Royal Highlander*. As usual for the time of year, all trains were very busy, and bad weather played a part in proceedings. In fact, our train home was so late on the Thursday morning that we worked a two-coach special hauled by **27055** (with its boiler working sweetly, too) as the main train, and its locomotive **47410** was at least 180 minutes late. After enjoying 25 and 26 December off, my year ended on ballast trains around the station area. Modernisation was sweeping away the mechanical signalling and, along with track rationalisation, the whole of the station and its approaches were up for some big changes. During a non-eventful week, trips pottering around **26010/27053** and **37260** kept a young man gainfully employed.

JACK 'THE BAT' FRASER CONTEMPLATES HIS NEXT MOVE DROPPING BALLAST. TAKEN AT GARVE IN 1984.

A YOUNG ALWYN ROSS PUSHES 26025 BACK OFF THE FUEL ROAD. WHAT LOOKS LIKE HIS DRIVER STEVIE LEWIS ON THE GROUND BACK TO CAMERA.

Chapter 5 - A Driver At Last

The start of a new year always seemed to bring out the need to do something different in my life. In 1985, it was to buy my own home. In 1986, it was to take a part-time job as a barman. Here in 1987, it felt time to move away from Inverness to pastures new. The railway I had joined had mostly gone, the characters who taught me the ropes were retiring one by one, and now we had drivers from down south taking all our jobs. It was time I took someone else's job and fought fire with fire. The promotion and transfer arrangements (PT&R) of the time allowed someone who left a depot on promotion, to register to return at their new grade at the first available opportunity. So, if I registered such a move when I left, it would prevent any driver from down south taking a job at Inverness until after I had returned, when my seniority allowed it. Redundancy moves overruled this.

With at least 15 passed drivers waiting for permanent driver's positions at the depot, my move blocked anyone coming back, including me, until all 15 had become drivers. So, all I had to do was find a depot that would have me, as my seniority date of February 1980 was years behind many others in the industry looking for jobs. The January vacancy list showed I was eligible for a move to Ayr, Yoker, Kirkdale or Manchester Victoria. I wanted to remain in Scotland and still drive locomotives, and not just multiple units. Ayr was the only depot that fitted the bill and ticked all those non-negotiable boxes. With the recent electrification of the mainline to Glasgow, ten new drivers' posts had been created, to reflect the enhanced train service. So, my application was submitted, and a nervous couple of weeks followed, pending a decision. At the time, all BR driver transfers and promotions were administered from York. Any letter with a York postcode was eagerly anticipated. Thankfully, in due course, the letter arrived. It informed me that my application was successful, and that my transfer date to Ayr would be on 22 February.

The timing was perfect, as another round of single manning was to take effect from 19 January. The role of the driver's assistant would be reduced to a bit player, with only a handful of mainline jobs and ballast work left. I may have been the first to leave, but I wasn't going to be the last.

However, Inverness wasn't quite done with me yet. On 12 January, I was given a driving turn on the *Clansman* service. The Perth men, who would normally work the turn, were delayed by heavy snow on the Highland line, so Alistair Macintyre and I took **47562** and the twelve coaches to Moy, before returning to Inverness with **47503**, on a very late and ice-bound *Royal Highlander*, We finally arrived in Inverness just before midday, almost four hours late, with a very weary trainload of passengers.

My good fortune continued, as next day, I was the driver of **37114**, due to the 1205 from Wick, which was being worked by **37420/37114** in tandem. After these highs, the rest of the month became a whole series

of lasts. Final trips to Kyle with **37420**, Burghead with **47641**, Invergordon with **37262** and Brora with **37419** and **37420** all took place with good humour, and what remained of some excellent mates from the start of my career. Eventually, my final shift arrived. Saturday 14 February brought a 0355 book for a trip to Aberdeen and back, with driver Manson Milne and **47550**. Booking off at 1055 brought down the curtain on seven years and two weeks of working with some excellent railway men, in a wonderful part of the world. Much had been learned, and would no doubt stand me in good stead going forwards. Following a hearty handshake from the TCS, Jock Robertson, I walked out the gate without looking back.

I was dropped off in Ayr by my family on Sunday 23 February. The big adventure was about to begin. I walked along the sea front, looking out towards the Isle of Arran, and prepared myself for all that lay ahead. At 0800 the next morning, I walked down the steps from Tams Brig as a fully-fledged BR driver for the very first time. The good thing was they knew that I was coming..After meeting the management and supervisory staff on duty, I was left in the care of one of the local ASLEF people for the rest of the morning. The chairman of the LDC was a former Hurlford driver called Tom Graham. He was a staunch socialist and was originally from the small mining town of Mauchline. This, of course, was the birthplace of Jimmy Knapp, who went on the lead the National Union of Rail Workers (NUR) before his untimely death in 2001. Tom and his colleague Bob Smilie gave me a warm welcome and a tour of the depot, along with a pep talk on how things were done, and the standards they expected of me as an ASLEF man. If I had been in any doubt that things were different here than at Inverness, these wise gentleman left me in no doubt that this place was run with a rod of iron.

The depot structure itself was much bigger than I had left behind up north, although strangely no mainline locomotives were allocated to Ayr. For the first time in my career, I was about to experience the railway linking structure and its peculiarities and perceived unfairness. At the time, Ayr had six links, with Link 1 being for senior drivers, and Link 4 the most junior. Links 5 and 6 were for restricted drivers who could only perform certain duties or shifts for medical reasons. As may be expected, I was the most inexperienced driver, and went to the very bottom of Link 4. The good thing was all the depot routes were shared throughout the links, although the junior links had the more unsocial turns of duty, along with all the different types of traction needed to work these trains. As a consequence, my route knowledge covered Glasgow via Paisley and Barrhead, Largs, Ardrossan, Stranraer, Carlisle via Dumfries, Hunterston and Polmadie, along with all the remaining freight terminals and opencast sites in the west of Scotland. Later, this route knowledge would be expanded to include Glasgow Works, Carstairs and Mossend Yard, via the infamous Rutherglen & Carmyle lines. Class 08, 20, 26,27,37,47, DMU and Class 318 electrics all went on my traction card. Some of these I already knew from Inverness.

It soon became clear that my fellow drivers and other staff involved in running the railway were very different to what I had been used to at Inverness. The depot was mostly crewed with people who had been born and bred in Ayrshire. Many of the more senior men had moved to Ayr following the closure of sheds such as Hurlford and Ardrossan. Others had come to live by the coast from places like Bridgeton, and other depots which closed as part of the Strathclyde manning agreement, and the opening of the super depot at Yoker in the early 1980s. It was a mixture of hard men who worked hard and played hard. No quarter was asked for or given. I knew immediately that as a soft-spoken Highlander, I would have to work very hard at fitting in. "Fit in or f*ck off," as the saying goes.

During all my time at Ayr, and indeed throughout all my footplate years, mostly the management I came into contact with can best be described as "firm but fair". The Train Crew Manager was a chap by the name of Alistair Smith, and a better boss it would be almost impossible to find. His Traction Inspector and chief tormentor of drivers was a young ambitious man called Eddie Carr. 'Big Eddie', as we called him, had a bark much worse than his bite. He would never go out of his way to trap you, and always let you know when he was about. At the shed itself, five train crew supervisors and the steel-eyed Roster Clerk, Craig Robertson, kept us is in check real time. In the main, they were all good guys in their own way, although some were more tyrannical than others.

Sensibly, my route learning was broken into chunks, and a programme was put together which looked like this:

- Glasgow, Largs and Ardrossan, including Corkerhill and Shields Road depots.

- Stranraer.

- Ayr harbour.

- Dumfries, including the Knockshinnoch branch.

- Carlisle station and yards.

Both Glasgow Central and Carlisle involved the use of a route learning instructor. Due to availability for Carlisle, it was agreed that any driving south of Dumfries would be route conducted, until this facility became available. In fact, Carlisle was the last route on my card to get signed off, and that wasn't until 13 August.

After some months driving to consolidate my knowledge, further training was provided as follows:

- Glasgow Works via the City Union lines.

- Mossend Yard via R&C.

- Polmadie depot.

- Killoch branch.

- East Kilbride and the Hamilton circle.

Traction was slightly less complicated, but only just. With some tractions already signed, the programme looked like this:

Class 318 EMU, three weeks. This was undertaken at Corkerhill, under the instruction of Tam Boag, who coincidentally happened to be a fellow Invernesian. The training consisted of two weeks in the classroom, looking at the technical aspects of the train, and a course in basic electricity, and all the dangers working with such equipment could bring. This was followed by a week out on the road, practising driving skills and train preparation duties, plus the all-important revision on the layout of all equipment.

DMU, three weeks. This was undertaken at Eastfield, in the north side of the city. This was a wild place inhabited by even wilder men than those from Ayrshire, or so it seemed to me.

The classroom itself was adjacent to the shed outlet signal and was fully equipped with an almost full-scale model of the drive train equipment of the DMU fleet. This training involved a week in the classroom learning about sun and planet wheels, sliding dogs and final drives, before a further two weeks out on the road, practising gear changes and driving this unique and highly pleasurable form of traction.

Class 20, two-day conversion from class 37. This was undertaken on Ayr TMD by one of the local driver instructors.

Class 26, one-day conversion from class 27. This was undertaken on Ayr TMD by one of the local driver instructors.

My first driving turn was on Turn 64. This involved booking on at 1525 and working the 1600 DMU to Girvan. I vividly recall bringing the empty Class 107 off shed, looking over at the empty seat next to me, and thinking, "gulp! I'm on my own here". The work content of the whole diagram involved a couple of trips to Girvan, and then Stranraer and back with the 1928 from Ayr, and return with the 2115. Empties to the shed and done by 2300 hours. Thankfully, as it was June and almost mid-summer, the trip to Stranraer was undertaken in almost total daylight, and peering out into the inky blackness would have to wait for the winter months. The same job was undertaken for the next couple of days, with the same Strathclyde-liveried Class 107. The week ended with the 2200 shed shunt.

For some reason, the link I was in had more than its fair share of work to Carlisle via Kilmarnock and Dumfries. We had the following turns of duty:

- 1055 Stranraer to Euston and back passenger via Glasgow C, Monday only.

- 1555 Stranraer to Tees and back with 6S66.

- 2200 Stranraer to Euston and back with the Brent to Stranraer (6S75).

- Pass via Glasgow Central for 1S06, Mondays only.

Just like Stranraer, the G&SW was one of my favourite roads to drive over. After clattering through Kilmarnock, the power would be fully applied, ready for the 18-mile climb to Polquap summit. Hulford signals would normally be off, as the box only opened on the rare occasions that trains needed to enter the distillery at Barleith. After crossing the Cessnock water twice, the train would roar through the 680-yard Mossgiel tunnel and through the small station at Mauchline, with the direct line from Ayr trailing in from the right, after coming up through Annbank. After finally staggering over the 600-foot summit, your train picked up speed as it raced downhill through Kirkconnel, Sanquhar and Thornhill, towards the first town of any size at Dumfries. However, before then, the train had crossed the magnificent Portrack viaduct over the River Nith, and passed the impressive-sounding signal box at Hollywood. On the final run into Dumfries, trains would pass the junction with the former Port Road from Stranraer. You can take the man out of the Highlands, but you can't take the Highlands out of the man.

Upon departure from Dumfries, we would blast along over the fast 70mph straight towards Ruthwell and Cummertrees, before passing through Annan station and onto the single-track section towards Gretna. Once clear of Gretna junction, the WCML from Glasgow would be joined for the final nine-mile section into the border city of Carlisle. This was a wonderful scenic journey, taking in hills, numerous viaducts and tunnels – signs of our industrial past – and finally, the 90mph dash over the edge of the debatable lands and into Carlisle itself.

Much of my route-learning to Carlisle was done in the company of Carlisle driver John Nattrass. John was an ex-canal man who came from a family of butchers. In fact, at the time of writing, the family still has a butcher's shop in Carlisle market. John was a thoroughly decent chap, and was more than happy to share his experiences with a willing young driver. It certainly made learning the road much easier. The last time I saw John was in 1988, when I relieved him at Ayr with 1S06 the 'Night Paddy'.

Another Carlisle-based character I have fond memories of is TCS Ray Gibson. Ray also had a calm approach to his work, and often appeared totally at ease, even if he had numerous problems to deal with at the same time. He would stand in the train crew lobby in his blue dustcoat, and calmly but firmly tell you what he wanted done. Even with the whole WCML falling apart around him, his demeanour never changed. He was definitely one of those people it was hard to say no to, and a fine and knowledgeable railway man – just another example of all that is missing. A story I remember best about Ray involved my one and only footplate trip on a Class 31. I had arrived in Carlisle with **47555** on the up 'Night Paddy'. By rights, I should have worked back with a Speedlink, not arriving in Ayr until almost 0800. I was more than delighted when Ray asked me to work back with the 3S07 parcels at 0250. Apparently, the Ayr driver for this train was running late, and would take my 6S55 instead. I collected **26027** from the wall side and backed down onto the three vans after they were detached from the main train 1S07 and shunted into Platform 1. The 26 must have suffered from a reverser fault, as try as I might, the locomotive would not reverse direction onto the stock. With my locomotive also blocking Platform 3, the *Royal Highlander* was also marooned in the border city. Once being made aware of the problem, Ray acted quickly to get me relieved by a local driver and my engine taken towards Kingmoor, in the only direction it seemed comfortable travelling. A grubby Class 31 was hijacked from a set of Gateshead men, and placed onto the now engineless and late 3S07. Of course, Ayr men did not sign such traction, so an equally grubby conductor driver was found to accompany me on this filthy heap. We headed off into the night with the 31 sounding as if was pulling at least 13 vehicles, and not our actual three. We huffed and puffed up hill and down dale, with hardly a word being spoken between us. The collective torture ended upon arrival in Ayr, just before 0500. After the shunter had done his work, the silent driver slipped away into the night and back to Carlisle with his noisy steed. Lasting impression of a Class 31? Not much, to be honest, and certainly no better than our own lesser-powered Type 2s.

It wasn't just little engines and parcels trains which could cause grief. 'Up' and 'Down Paddy' boat trains were always good for at least one farce, every once in a while. With connections with sailings to and from Ireland, and trains running over the congested WCML from the south, on-time running was the exception, and not the norm. Slick locomotive changes would help claw back some lost time, but leaving Carlisle anything up to 20 minutes late was deemed a success.

The mess room at Carlisle was the perfect place to people-watch. It brought together Jocks and English, east and west, all into a single melting pot. The banter was mostly good natured, but if any 'foreign' driver happened to win the jackpot on the one-armed bandit, then things could quickly turn ugly. The room was divided into several smaller rooms, with an English and Scottish section both segregated by a wall, and a couple of one-armed bandits. In the very back was a small, quiet room. This was the ideal place to get your head down for an hour or so, as well as being the lair of the infamous Polmadie man, Basher Bates. Even in the English room, the Geordies kept themselves to themselves, as did the Preston men, and those from the smaller West Cumbrian depots, such as Workington and Barrow.

After the Stranraer to Euston day-time 'Paddy' had ceased to be an InterCity service and became instead a regional railways Class 156, we used to work Ayr to Carlisle only, and then home passenger via Glasgow Central. More often than not, the guard and I would ride in the passenger accommodation, though occasionally with permission, in the driving cab of the Class 86/2 or 87. Compared with our diesel slog out of Carlisle, flying north on an electric, with the speedo touching 90mph as we passed Kingmoor yard a little over four miles out, was miles ahead of anything I had experienced thus far. Flying along with **87023**, the nose end covered in fly squash as we totally demolished Beattock Bank with a late running

CrossCountry service is a memory that will never leave me. It really captured the spirit of the time as the Glasgow driver did all he could to win back minutes lost further south.

THE LARNE FERRY STEAMS INTO PORT ON **14/5/86** READY TO OFF LOAD ANOTHER LOAD OF PASSENGERS FOR ONWARDS TRAIN CONNECTIONS.

THE NIGHT PADDY AFTER ARRIVAL IN STRANRAER. OUR PASS RIDE HOME AT **0700** IS SEEN IN THE ADJACENT PLATFORM.

Stranraer had at least two daily freights in each direction at this time. Both mostly conveyed Northern Irish traffic, with all freight using the handling facility at Stockton Haulage, on the former branch line to Portpatrick. The traffic would be taken the short distance to/from the harbour by road. The only exception I can remember is car traffic, which was tripped to the harbour by shunting engine, and loaded straight onto the ship's quayside. Most of the freight trains were well loaded, and it would be a struggle to lift heavy trains of 600 tons plus up Glendoune or the swan's neck, especially on a greasy rail.

The 'Paddy' used to leave Ayr at 0406 in the morning, to connect with the first steamer to Larne. The train loaded to about seven vehicles, and in autumn, had a pilot engine to help with adhesion on the fierce hills beyond Girvan. With a good run and fair weather, the train would arrive in the port a little after 0600. After a cup of tea with the sleeping car attendant, we would travel back passenger on the first Stranraer to Glasgow train, arriving back in Ayr for 0830. After I moved into the town centre, I could be home in bed by 0900, with a whole day to enjoy, after my second sleep.

6S75 was a different matter. It had a later booking on at 0710, and would pass the 1055 London train at Dunragit. This meant that with no back working, the driver of this one-man operated DOO train would be marooned in Stranraer for almost five hours, with no way of getting back to Ayr. With hindsight, I should have spent the time exploring this wonderful part of Scotland. However, more often than not, I walked out to the main A77 road and thumbed a lift back to Ayr. I often joked with the driver who finally stopped to pick me up that I had lost my locomotive, and was being sent back to get another one. Many a motorist must have thought British Railways employed some rather stupid people, if they could manage to misplace a large blue locomotive.

Considering the remote and rural nature of the area, the railways to Stranraer have carried significant amounts of freight traffic down the years. During both wars, massive tonnages of freight and people would cram into packed carriages to get to where they needed to be, with creature comforts playing little part in the proceedings. In the early 1920s, the first vehicle-carrying ferries crossed the North Channel, making Stranraer a credible port for the Irish market. This allowed the movement of animals and dairy produce, for example, all the way from the farm to the railhead, before being loaded onto the train for forward transit.

I am also led to believe that at one point well into the 1960s, and no doubt replacing the long-standing Stranraer to Glasgow College Yard and return service, a daily Millerhill to Stranraer ran in each direction. This was the main way of getting household coal, animal feed, electrical goods and other household necessities from factory to consumer, along with milk, cheese and cattle from farm to market. The demise of vacuum-braked pick-up freights, along with the changing industrial landscape of the central belt, was once again the reason for this type of train becoming surplus to requirements. The train was worked by a Corkerhill crew who had a short nine-hour lodge in Stranraer, before returning north with the balancing evening service.

During World War Two at the height of the Blitz, the Churchill-led government decided they needed to build a new deep-water port, for use if enemy bombing incapacitated existing docks at Liverpool and Glasgow. Cairn Port on Loch Ryan was the preferred site, and in 1941, the building of Military Railway Number 2 commenced. The approximately six-mile line from Cairnryan Junction to the port finally opened in 1943, although by then, the tide of war was turning, and thankfully, the port was never fully utilised for its intended purpose. In any case, the LMS would have had great difficulty hauling additional freight tonnage over the big hills and fitting extra freights in among the large amount of Northern Irish troop traffic. Using the line would have required both routes to operate well in excess of their intended capacity.

Following the end of hostilities, the line to Cairn Point had a short secondary existence hauling unwanted munitions for disposal at sea in the deep waters of Beauforts Dyke, out in the North Channel. Almost 150,000 tons of munitions were dumped at the bottom of this 300m deep-sea dustbin, with a fair tonnage coming by rail. This traffic usually ran in trains of around 17 wagons via Girvan, or 30 wagons via Newton Stewart, and ran off/on for a period of around three years. It took a brave driver to thrash his steam engine up Glendoune or across the High Chain with sparks raining down from the heavens on the deadly cargo behind, but it was something the drivers of the day did, day in and day out.

For several years, there was also a spring lamb train from Glenwhilly to Carlisle. The wagons came empty via Falkland, and three wagons were loaded at a time between trains up at Glenwhilly. In addition, for several years, coal services ran by rail from the South Ayrshire pits at Bargany and Dalquarrin mines to Girvan harbour, for export to Ireland, along with Stranraer, for domestic use. This would have added to the frequency and variety of traffic south of Ayr. In more mundane times, most of the freight traffic running to Stranraer continued to be for onwards movement by sea to Northern Ireland. This posed its own problems:.the loaded trains really only operated one way, and therefore had significant amounts of empty mileage, which ultimately led to freight's demise on the route in the 1990s. To add to the inefficiency, all Irish traffic would need multiple handling, as the ferries ex Stranraer to Larne and return only had car decks. With Northern Ireland's rail network being passenger only, all onwards shipment was by road haulage. Additionally, with a high tide of only around four metres in Stranraer, the types of vessels used, limited the amount of cargo carried per crossing, even after frequent dredging of the channel in/out of the port. The Saint class ferries, namely *Caledonian Princess*, the *Antrim Princess*, the *Ailsa Princess*, and finally, the *Galloway Princess* all plied the short sea crossing at some point down the years, carrying passengers, freight and goods vehicles in all imaginable weather conditions.

New cars from Dagenham, Luton and Merseyside, steel products from Teesside/Workington and Taunton Cider, along with milk traffic from the numerous Galloway creameries, made up the main peacetime tonnages. Following the closure of the Port Road in 1965, all this traffic travelled the long way round, via Falkland and Girvan, placing great strain on the limited mountain infrastructure. This was even more so after the singling of the route from Dalrymple Junction to Girvan, in 1965. Any delay would quickly escalate, with crossing points missed and trains kept waiting for inbound locomotives and crew.

By the time I transferred to Ayr in 1987, as in other parts of Scotland, much of the freight traffic was no longer there to be moved, or had transferred to road haulage. The notorious A75 between Gretna and Stranraer was a known accident black spot, as HGV drivers drove hard to make the port for an onwards ferry connection. In fact, one of the bridges along this stretch carried the dubious honour of the most hit bridge by HGVs in the whole of Scotland. The remaining rail freight traffic ran in two Speedlink services, with 6S66 leaving Falkland at 0340, and 6S75 a few hours later at 0813. Because of the need for trains to be downloaded for the tortuous run south of Ayr, the above services would often be supplemented by a third train to Stranraer, leaving around 1000. This train would carry any traffic left behind by the booked trains, along with seasonal wagons of fertiliser, for use on the numerous Galloway farms.

The trains would arrive from Carlisle with a Class 37 or 47 in charge, depending on the load and length, as the 37 could only manage 950 tons over the G&SW, even when running in a slower 45mph Class seven path. From memory, 6S66 produced a Thornaby 47, far more often than not, and 6S75 a Class 37 from either Gateshead or Thornaby. Within minutes of arriving in Falkland, the shunters would tie off wagons not destined for Stranraer – no coupling on/off in this part of the world. This traffic would go forwards to its ultimate destination on one of the daytime trippers such as R02 or R05, to Dalry, Stevenson, Irvine or Kilmarnock. This usually left only cars and steel with the occasional VGA for the next leg. 6S66 was a Stranraer driver off the 'Night Paddy', and Ayr men would follow on behind several hours later, with 6S75. This was one of the jobs in my link, and one of the few day-shift jobs with a sociable 0730 book on time. So, let's have a trip with **37101** over the hills to the port.

After booking on and looking for my engine number on the loco board, it was case of collecting my bag from the locker room and climbing onto the 37, which had been fuelled and prepared by the shed driver. The short trip over to Falkland Yard via the cross over at Tams Brig and onto Number 2 reception road in the yard, before buffering up to the short train of two car carriers and three bogie steel wagons, gave all-up weight of around 380 tons. With the brake continuity test completed and all paperwork in order, the 37 was given an initial short burst of power to get things rolling, once authority had been given for us to proceed. The first Stranraer to Glasgow passenger train was passed on the double line section to Dalrymple Junction. After this, it was pretty much an empty railway, with no other traffic to cross until 1M06, the 'Day Paddy' at Dunragit. 6S75 had an arrival time in Stranraer at 1130, and after shunting his train, the driver would have several hours to kill, until his passenger ride home mid-afternoon. Some drivers, myself included, would enjoy a stroll around the small town, and a spot of lunch, before walking down to the harbour station, and a ride on the cushions home to Ayr. However, some of my more impatient colleagues would endeavour to thumb a lift from one of the vehicles arriving off the midday ferry. If successful, they would manage to get back to base before the diagrammed ride home had even left Stranraer. I did not try the hitch-hiking pass ride home myself, but I do remember some hilarious bothy humour and anecdotes from those that did. Driving freight trains over this underrated line took more skill than may first be imagined. The route from Ayr to Girvan has ever-changing gradients, and hardly a single mile of it is on level track. A freight made up of anything near the maximum length for the route of 1,200 feet would lead to difficult driving conditions. The front of the train could be going uphill while the back end was still on a downhill section. Rugs, tugs and a risk of broken couplings were a real and present risk. Moreover, on a greasy wet rail, a train could be bowling down Crosshill Bank, only to encounter Kilkerran distant at caution. A heavy application of the brake was needed almost immediately, as the line hugged the large Glensalloch Forest, and was therefore well shaded, and often extremely slippery. With the distant to home signal only providing minimum braking distance, toes could curl for anyone not thinking ahead at this location. After another potentially hairy descent of Killochan Bank, the train then passed the site of the once rail-served Grangeston munitions factory. Also known to locals as the 'secret works', this site was a thriving place of important war works, and even had its own station, served by a morning and evening workers' train to/from Ayr. Once through Girvan, the driver would need to thrash his locomotive up the 1:54/80/56 four-mile ramp of Glendoune Bank, past the Girvan waterworks, and out into open countryside, before plunging once again downhill through Pinmore Tunnel, and onto the dip at the token point at Pinwherry. Further hard pounding would follow up the 1:69 climb to Barrhill and another crossing or a nonstop, hand-over-hand token exchange, before the final twisting climb though the infamous Gunners Cuttin' to Chirmorie Summit at the 16.5 milepost, 863 above sea level, which was of course, last seen at Girvan. This was a hard enough task on a dry rail in daylight, and an even harder one on a dark stormy night, with little to guide a driver as to the train's exact whereabouts. Add in snow or autumn leaves, and you can perhaps begin to get a sense of cab workload being high and stressful, on anything other than a normal operating day. This was a wild and lonely 38 miles, and in many respects, was one of the hardest roads in Scotland to drive heavy trains over. It was certainly the last place I ever worked where the driver had to feel the road beneath him at night. With no other landmarks, a lurch to the left or right, with a slight change in speed, meant something, or required an adjustment to the power handle or brake controller. I suspect those who drove the West Highland Line regularly would empathise with this comment.

With all those 863 feet to be lost before Stranraer, the train would then experience a marked rate of descent as it followed the Water of Luce down to the token exchange point at Glenwhilly. This area is steeped in history, and nearby places such as the blood moss standing stones, added to the feeling of being somewhere off grid. After another short uphill stretch, 6S75 would once again plunge downhill, and around the infamous Swan's Neck reverse curves, and the nearest I have ever seen in the UK to an Alpine hill-hugging hill climb/descent. The 'Neck', as it was known to railway men, was a location where heavy trains coming in the opposite direction would first encounter deep snow as they climbed away from the sea at 1:57. In autumn, it was a location where the heavy boat trains would often slip to a stand. Running southbound, the brakes would be heating up nicely as 6S75 slowed for New Luce and the final five miles of downhill, onto more level ground at Dunragit, and your first glimpse of the sea at Luce Bay and, on a clear day, the Isle of Man beyond. An easy run would follow along the flat lands through Castle Kennedy, with its former WW2 airfield and torpedo plane training school. The brakes would go on hard for Stranraer Harbour junction, as it was at the bottom of a 1:86 descent, and into the ultimate destination of the Stockton Haulage yard, based at the stub end of the former Portpatrick branch, which was closed to all traffic in 1959. I was once told by a local driver that Portpatrick was the embarkation point for the original short sea crossing to Donaghadee, in Northern Ireland. The port only lost favour because it was susceptible to heavy seas on stormy days, and therefore unusable for long periods.

Both return freights from Stranraer had evening departures, allowing the traffic to be off-loaded during the day. Consequently, drivers from the former 68C shed were in charge, and Ayr men only took over at Falkland Yard for the evening run over the G&SW to Kingmoor Yard, in Carlisle. This was only fair, as the Stranraer men had lost so much work down the years, following the closure of the Port Road. In their eyes, the Ayr men had plenty of work on the flatter roads to Glasgow and farther afield.

The very nature of the traffic flows meant all the Speedlink services returning from Stranraer consisted of empty vehicles. In the eyes of the new sector management, they were therefore unprofitable, irrespective of how many HGV trips they kept off the A75/A77.

By the time I left Ayr, the writing was already on the wall, as Intercity pulled out of the Stranraer and G&SW routes in 1988, thus burdening ScotRail and Speedlink with the full costs of running this expensive-to-operate rural route. The national Speedlink review finally killed off daily freight traffic over Glendoune, and the final freights ran for the last time in the spring of 1992. The Stockton Haulage depot soon closed, as did the unloading pad for cars at the harbour. With all its traffic lost, the R32 pilot turn soon followed, and some further redundancies took place amongst the ever-dwindling ranks of Stranraer railwaymen. Moreover, the final curtain came down on another chapter of Glasgow & South Western history.

In hindsight, the once-buoyant freight service went into decline after the closure of the direct route to the south, with many of the traditional traffic flows ending, or transferring to road haulage. The traffic flows that did cling on did remarkably well to last for as long as they did. Certainly, those involved (me included) in operating freight trains the long way round via Ayr did a first-class job in meeting the customers' needs, often in difficult and challenging circumstances.

Let's get in our time machine and go back to a late summer morning in 1987. The lobby at Ayr is warm and welcoming, as were most train crew booking-on areas, with years of tobacco stains on the walls and ceilings, and hard polished floors which had seen generations of engine men come and go. Even at this early hour, a few people are about, either booking on duty or finishing a night shift, with banter and gossip exchanged, and the usual grumbles of shift workers. The foreman Doug McClure tells me 1S06 is running on time, so the working day is hopefully off to a good start. I read the late notices: 20mph ESR at Kilkerran is the only item of interest on today's trip. I collect my bag from the locker room and head out into the night and the 20-minute walk to the station, which will take me out past Somerset Park, home of Ayr United FC. I head over the bridge, past the bowling green and through the maze of houses at Kirktonholme, before crossing the river and approaching the station up Mill Street, as the first of the day's Class 318s set of empty to Largs for start of service.

With 1S06, or the 'Night Paddy', as we knew it, just coming off the single line from Kilmarnock at Barassie, I had time to fill my mash can in the supervisor's office, before going out onto Platform 3. The headlight of the Brush 4 came into view, as it crossed from down line to up line, on its approach to the station. The screeching of the ravenous gulls which always overflew the town at this unearthly hour was thankfully drowned out by the reassuring Sulzer beat, as **47604** drew to a halt beside me, at the head of its short six-coach train. The carriage lighting cast ghostly shadows on the platform, and the hum of the motor alternators made this well-filled train stand out as something different from the norm.

With the cab light turned on, it was possible to identify Carlisle driver John Nattrass, who had brought the train over the G&SW and would now pass to Glasgow C, to work the first Glasgow to Carlisle service, departing at 0725 back home. We exchanged control keys, and John shared the information that all was well with the loco, and I had six on for 215 tons – no train at all for a 2580hp locomotive. It was always a pleasure to see John, as he was one of the G&SW regulars who I had learned the road with. As would be expected from an old hand, he knew every inch of the railway between Gretna J and Ayr like the back of his hand. Bob Smilie at Ayr was one of the other old-hand drivers I did my route-learning to Stranraer with. Not only did he know every blade of grass over the route; he also told some fascinating tales of life on the line in steam days. He knew many of the fabled G&SW 'drivers wild' well, including possibly the most famous of them all, Bob McCann. McCann's good-natured boast was that the sparks from the chimney of his steamer flew so high as he thrashed the banks that they were still falling back to earth when he was on the return trip. John and Bob were the kind of drivers you could listen to all day long, and never get bored.

1S06 had five minutes' station time to off load newspapers and mail, so by the time station work was completed, my first mug was pretty much drained. The signal at the end of the platform winked to green to signify the crossing at Belmont was down, and the section to Dalrymple Junction clear. I received the Right Away and closed my fist around the large red and silver power handle. I felt the reassuring surge in amps, as the 47 lifted the 'Paddy' and the mostly still-slumbering occupants out into the night.

After passing over Belmont crossing, I usually looked over to the left at the house of my soon-to-be in-laws in Kincaidston, noting the house was still in total darkness, as you'd expect at this early hour. The streetlights of Ayr were left behind, as we picked up speed and climbed out into open countryside, with the speedo climbing through the 50s towards 60mph. At the top of the bank, the freight-only line to

Dalmellington opencast continued its climb away from the sea, while the port line dipped downhill and out of the control of Paisley Signalling Centre into Tokenless block signalling territory. **47604** rolled us through Maybole, the ancient capital of the Kingdom of Carrick, and not many miles away from Alloway, the birthplace of the ploughman poet, Rabbie Burns. I always thought of one of his favourite quotes, when driving on this road: "There is no such uncertainty as a sure thing".

This may come as a surprise to many, but the railway between Maybole, and the train's first stop at Girvan, is one of the hardest in the UK over which to drive. The route, which was built by the G&SW on a shoestring, is like a sawtooth, with the gradient constantly changing, and barely a mile of it on the level. It really is a driver's railway, and must have been a total nightmare in the days of unbraked Class 9 freights. On certain stretches, a long freight train would be on three different gradients at once. With such featherweight trains as 1S06, it was just a case of keeping the train rolling smoothly at 60mph, and focusing as much on passenger comfort as anything else. Not forgetting, of course, the 20mph speed restriction at Kilkerran – a location frequently troubled with embankment slippage, even to this day.

The 'Paddy' was booked to stand at Girvan from 0441/0446, before the real hard work of the day began: the four-mile climb of Glendoune Bank, initially at 1:54 before easing to 1:80, past the Girvan waterworks, followed by a final 1:56 slog to the 394 foot summit at Pinmore. Not high, in the scheme of things, but when you think that Girvan is at sea level, then almost 100 feet of elevation per mile is some going, and a real test of any traction, at any time of year. We had now entered electric token territory, so with the tablet for Pinwherry on board, it was time to climb some hills. Pretty much from the end of the platform, the gradient hits us at 1:54, and the big brush was worked extremely hard, and never above 30mph all the way up the hill. With the first light of dawn now kicking in, the massive bulk of Ailsa Craig could be seen away to the right, standing guard over the Firth of Clyde. This huge volcanic plug of granite stands ten miles out to sea, and had the local nickname of 'Paddy's milestone', possibly to let anyone who was on the road to Stranraer, know that the end was near. The rasp of the exhaust carried on the breeze, as we twisted and turned ever higher into the hills, and further from any form of urbanisation. We plunged into Pinmore tunnel, as the almost model-sized tunnel mouth swallowed us up, and for a few brief moments, the train vanished under the hill. After passing over the stone viaduct at Kinclair, the power handle was fully closed, and the steep descent into Pinwherry began. Pinwherry still had a box and passing loop, but the station itself had closed on 6 September 1965, no doubt as a precursor to the whole line closing as part of the good Doctor's reshaping of Britain's railways. Thankfully, it didn't, but the other Port Road, over the High Chain via Newton Stuart to Dumfries, was sacrificed instead. With no trains to pass at this early hour, we passed through the loop. After taking the Pinwherry to Barrhill token on board, the power handle was pulled wide open for the almost continuous four-mile climb to the line's only remaining intermediate station. The 47 coped well on the climb, and speed balanced at around 30mph, with 4,000 amps being pushed down to the six traction motors.

1S06 wasn't booked to stop at Barrhill, and with the station situated in the middle of nowhere, right on the edge of the massive Galloway Forest, custom was sparse, to say the least, even at the best of times. Occasionally, weather permitting, I took my racing bike up to Barrhill by train, before cycling the 60-70 miles back to Ayr via Straiton, Patna and the superbly named Nick o' the Balloch. Following a brief chat with the signaller, as I slowed to nothing more than walking pace for the token exchange, we were off again, with the final climb to the line's summit at Chirmorrie, 690 feet above sea level, and as dark and wild a place as I have ever seen in the whole of the UK. The Chirmorrie had no real railway connection historically, other than a couple of railway cottages near the summit. The name itself came from a large shooting lodge across the moor to the east. Once you had passed the Barrhill distant signal, you had eleven miles of empty land to cross. If that wasn't enough, the approach to the summit from either side was over open moorland, and via a series of reverse curves. The largest of these, between Glenwhilly and New Luce, is better known as the swan's neck, due to the almost S-shaped pattern the railway took as it hugged the hillside on its descent into the passing loop and former station of Glenwhilly. This location was only accessible by a long, unmetalled track from the old military road crossing the moor. After another token exchange, it's more downhill ski slope freewheeling round the swan's neck, and down the 1:57 section, over the very substantial Main Water of Luce viaduct, past the site of the former New Luce station, and onto flatter lands and the Port Road proper at Challoch Junction, the site of the much-lamented route from Dumfries trailed in on the down side. The final token exchange took place at Dunragit and its passing loop, before a fast run into Stranraer, with the speedo hovering at 60-65mph along the long flat straight track, close to the A75 road.

The approach to the town itself was slow and tortuous, with a 20mph curve past the site of the former town station, steam shed and Stair Park, the home of Stranraer FC. After running along the back of the high street, the line went onto a causeway out to the harbour itself. Journey's end saw **47604** dwarfed alongside the Belfast-built *MV Galloway Princess*, as we came to a halt in Platform 2. The large white ship was prepared for her next sea crossing over the fabled short sea route to Larne. As our mostly ferry-bound weary passengers ambled sleepy-eyed after a night in a warm Mark 2 or 3 coach, the journey of over 450 miles from London was at an end.

As for me, it was a case of handing 604 over to the Stranraer driver (quite possibly a Tweedie, as many rail staff in Stranraer carried that name), to shunt the train up to the old town station for servicing. Then it was time for a quick freshen up, home passenger on the 0700 back to Ayr, and back home, before most of the world had even woken up.

Fast forwards six months and 15 hours, to a February night in 1988, as we once again find ourselves on the causeway, this time with a three-car Ayr-based Class 107 DMU which would shortly be working the 2115 service to Ayr, and a connection into the last Glasgow EMU at 2300. The 1800 sailing from Larne was late, so, as was custom and practice back then, our train was to be held, to make sure the Glasgow connection was made.

The lights of the 10,000-ton vessel could soon be seen steaming past Kirkcolm point and up Loch Ryan. All being well, we would be on our way by 2120. It had been a wild and windy trip from Ayr with the 1928 service, so I wasn't optimistic at all about our chances of making up the lost time on the return trip.

The DMU was a new traction for me, as they had all left Inverness by the time I joined the railway in 1980. So, let me give a brief explanation of what was in front of me, and how this type of traction was driven.

To my left was a row of air and axle lights, with a pair illuminated for each vehicle in this three-car set. The lights told the driver that the engines on that vehicle were running, the reversing 'dogs' were set for the direction you wished to travel in, and finally, that a minimum of 75psi of air pressure was available.

Below the lights was a power controller, including the Deadman's handle. Beside my right hand was the gear selector with gears 1-4, and also the reversing handle, which set the transmission to the direction of travel selected by the driver.

In front of me under the large windscreen left to right was the speedo, tachometer for engine revs, vacuum brake gauges, and finally, the main air supply gauge.

Scattered around all the above were the AWS display and button, lighting and heating switches, handbrake and finally, the warning horn.

The driving technique for a DMU was fairly technical, and great damage could be done to the transmission and engines if not adhered to. In layman's terms:

With the engines at idle, the driver would select first gear and release the brakes in one single movement.

The power controller would then be moved to full power and the tachometer observed until change gear was indicated. The power controller would then be moved to off and, after a four-second delay to allow the revs to drop off, second gear would then be selected. The same procedure would be followed until fourth gear was reached, and this gear would also be used for coasting purposes.

When approaching a gradient, fourth gear would be maintained until engines revs fell off, or the train reached 41mph and the change down indicator on the tachometer informed the driver a lower gear was needed.

When it came to stopping, once again, things needed to be done properly, as the Gresham and Craven quick-release vacuum brake system was very different to loco-hauled stock.

The brake valve must be applied quickly and without pausing in the lap position. The lap was only used when the desired brake application had been achieved and in lap, it would be held at this rate of retardation, until further action was required by the driver.

The final brake application before coming to a stand would be held in lap until about 10mph, when the gear selector would be placed in neutral, and the brake fully released, before returning to lap just before the train came to a graceful halt.

All this was highly effective if done properly, but great damage to the equipment or embarrassment to the driver could be done, if there was any deviation from the standard operating procedure.

The signaller brought me the Dunragit token and, after exchanging a few pleasantries, he retreated to the warmth of his box on Platform 2. Now, all that remained was to wait for the few hardy souls off the ferry to join us. Once I had received 2 on the buzzer, as the 'right away' signal from our guard, Willie Michaels, we were off. Running along the causeway, we passed the stock for the 'Night Paddy' being readied to come down into the station once we had cleared the causeway. The old rattler was slowly but surely gunned up, and put into third gear for the 1:86 climb past the former Cairn Ryan military railway junction. A thick haze of acrid exhaust was spread over the town, as the engines of the Strathclyde-liveried 107 cleared their respective throats, after many minutes of idling in the station.

In daylight hours, I always ran my DMU with the blinds up, to allow interested passengers a view of the line ahead. However, on a dark night such as this, it was out of the question, as the glare from the saloon lights would make forwards visibility for the driver almost impossible. So, for the next 90 minutes or so, I would be cocooned in my own little world.

Speed picked up on the downhill section past Castle Kennedy, and we rattled along in fourth gear at 60mph, with everything imaginable shaking and rattling, despite this particular DMU being classed as a

Derby Heavyweight unit. The Driving Motor Composite with Lavatory (DMCL) in which we were currently sat in, weighed in at around 32 tons. With the typical soft suspension of this kind of unit, we rocked and rolled over the 60-foot lengths of jointed track, with a comforting clickety clack as we passed over each rail joint.

The next obstacle to be overcome was the token exchange at Dunragit. With this type of traction, the driver needed a minimum of three hands to be able to do the exchange on the move. Let me explain: we approached Dunragit at 20mph, with the brake on for the token exchange at 10mph, 100 yards or so ahead. I had the Stranraer to Dunragit token in my left hand. I needed to keep my right hand free to collect the Dunragit to Glenwhilly token, and with my improvised third hand, I had to blow off the brake, while at the same time keeping the throttle-operated driver's safety device depressed. I won't go into the nitty-gritty of how it was done, as several techniques could be deployed to ensure nothing was dropped, along with the driver's dignity being maintained. 99 times out of 100, it was successfully undertaken, and on the very odd occasion, a token was dropped, then an emergency brake application was needed, before sheepishly walking back to collect it. Or, if the large leather pouch had bounced off into the undergrowth or cracked the signaller on the shin, a search for the offending article could take several minutes, including profuse apologies to the aggrieved signaller.

There was a longing look to the right at the formation of the port road running off towards Glenluce and beyond. Then the climbing of the big hill began, initially at 1:78, but soon stiffening to a gear-crunching 1:57 round the swan's neck, with the old railcar by now toiling in second gear at a little over 20mph, as we climbed higher into the night, with our small group of passengers no doubt looking forward to the fact that their long journey would soon be ending, whatever their reasons for travelling on a dark winter's night.

The token exchange at Glenwhilly once again required the octopus technique, with arms flailing, knee on the DSD, before hauling the Barrhill token aboard, then winding on the power for the four-mile climb to the line's summit at Milepost 16.5. The darkness up here was intense, as the wind blew a strong sou'westerly, sending the clouds racing over the sky, with fleeting glimpses of the upwards-pointing crescent moon adding to the sense of mid-winter total isolation. It was certainly no night to be out at sea on the north channel.

The approach to Barrhill from the south was, if anything, worse than the north. It was approached by a number of reverse curves with only the feel of the rails underneath you to guide you through the inky blackness. Meanwhile, your eyes strained for a first glimpse of the distant signal and the hoped-for security of a green lamp, to tell you the section ahead was clear. Back in the old days, I was told by Andy Keegan that the inhabitants of the cottages would place a detonator on the rail, if they required a train to stop for an unauthorised and impromptu trip to Girvan or beyond. There was no patronage tonight at Barrhill, but at least an opportunity to exchange tokens stationary, along with a blether with the signaller, before the downwards 65mph plunge to sea level, via the hump at Pinmore summit. We fairly flew down the hill to Pinwherry, past the farmhouse known as 'the sixpence', for some strange and long-forgotten reason, by the banks of the River Stinchar. The last and final upwards 1:69 slog for Pinmore was the only real challenge remaining. It was a climb that our veteran Class 107 must have done hundreds of times before, but not for much longer, as all the sets would be transferred away from Ayr later in 1988, when the Class 156 super sprinters took over all such workings.

The descent of Glendoune was always spectacular on this train, as we flew downhill at 60mph past the water works and into the station, with a whoosh of vacuum brakes and just a hint of a jolt, as we stopped serenely, as long as the braking had been judged to the necessary precision. This was great stuff, and all part of the joys of driving this particular type of traction.

We had safely arrived back in a more populated part of Ayrshire. As a consequence, we had custom at both Girvan and, after climbing Crosshill Bank, also at Maybole. Then we enjoyed a final 70mph gallop down the hill from Dalrymple and into Ayr station, on time to the minute, with all arrears recovered, thanks to some good old-fashioned teamwork.

The departing passengers either made their way out of the station, or over to Number 2 bay platforms, for an easy connection into the last Glasgow EMU service of the day.

With Willie Michaels based at the station, it was a solo DOO trip to the depot for me. Once the Glasgow train had departed, I followed in a cloud of hazy blue exhaust for the next and final stop: Ayr TMD. The old workhorse was put to bed and I was off duty and walking home.

A CLASS 101 AT GIRVAN IN AUGUST 1989. IN MY LINK WE WOULD DO 2 ROUND TRIPS FROM AYR THEN STRANRAER AND BACK ALL WITH THE SAME UNIT. 101 304 WAS ONE OF MY REGULARS.

STRANRAER TOWN YARD IN BUSIER TIMES. THE R32 PILOT AWAITS SOME CUSTOM COPYRIGHT HARRY ARCHIBALD.

THE INFAMOUS GLENDOUNE BANK AS SEEN FROM A DEPARTING 40 HAULED RAIL TOUR.

OLD SCHOOL AT KILMARNOCK. COPYRIGHT RAIL-ONLINE.CO.UK

CLASS 318 AT GLASGOW CENTRAL. GREAT UNITS AND ABLE TO RUN AT 100MPH WHEN RUNNING LATE.

BUSY SCENE AT CARLISLE. BUT THEN AGAIN THEY ALL WERE BACK THEN.

READY FOR ANOTHER DAY COAL CRUNCHING. 2x20'S DROP OFF SHED TO FALKLAND YARD.

Local passenger work

Two of the most-avoided jobs at the depot involved multiple trips over the same route. The most despised of these involved five round trips between Ayr and Girvan. In the days before the industry measured fatigue levels of its drivers, shifts like this were pure torture. At times, you would forget which trip you were on, and it was not uncommon to chance ends at Ayr and go back again, only to be told by the guard that this was our meal break, and the next trip wasn't for an hour.

The other shift I remember from all those years ago was turn 88. This involved booking on at 0700. The first train worked was the 0715 to Glasgow, followed by the 0830 back to Ayr, 0945 back to Glasgow, meal break 1035-1120, 1145 down to Largs, 1330 back to Glasgow and finally the 1500 home to Ayr. Total brain death, and with next to no stimulation on a solid Class 318, DOO day.

We also had DMU work on both the East Kilbride and Barrhead routes, with an occasional train continuing on to Kilmarnock, supplementing the two-hour loco-hauled service to Carlisle, covered by either Carlisle or Corkerhill men. However, at least you changed gear on a DMU, and no unit was the same as the next one.

The DMU service used the bay platforms in Kilmarnock, and picked up the next non-loco-hauled standard path to Glasgow. Trains called at Kilmaurs, Stewarton, Dunlop and Barrhead, before running fast to Glasgow. The hourly Barrhead terminators, of which we had our fair share, picked up at the smaller stations, such as Nitshill and Kennishead. This route was also used to move DMUs to/from Ayr for maintenance, and therefore kept the elderly vehicles away from the busy route via Paisley.

One job always guaranteed to be fun was the 2315 Glasgow Central to Kilmarnock, and the empty to Ayr. The train would often run with nine vehicles, albeit with only a three-car in use for passengers. On Saturday 14 November 1987, I left the Central with a nine-car, with most of the vehicles in the set carrying some kind of defect. As I climbed the Shilford bank between Barrhead and Lugton, I began to lose engines one by one. I staggered over the summit, and thankfully began to pick up speed on the descent towards Stewarton. By this time, I was down to three engines running, and six dead. As I began to make my brake application for the station, I forgot one simple fact of DMU operation: the exhausters for the braking system were driven off the engine. So, no engine meant a much slower application of the brake. With only 33% of the engines running, I knew straight away that I wasn't going to stop – well, not in the platform anyway. One by one, the vehicles passed sedately through the platform, until I finally ground to a halt with only the rear vehicle still in the station. After conferring with the guard, Willie Michaels, we decided the best course of action was to take the hapless group of over-carried, and in many cases intoxicated, passengers all the way to Kilmarnock for taxis back. Unfortunately for me, a vacuum brake that was slow to apply was even slower to release, and it took many minutes before I had sufficient vacuum to move the train. I arrived in Kilmarnock station, I had a red face as I changed ends, and scurried off back to Ayr via Barassie. After a long shift, I finally arrived in number 1 road of the shed with a single engine still running, and lots of throttle for sufficient brake to keep the wheels turning.

Local freight work

Ayr was predominantly a freight depot, although much of its former work had ended with the decimation of the coal industry, following the miners' strike of 1984. The coal that remained was taken from opencast sites, with the vast majority being sent to Kilroot power station in Northern Ireland, carried by way of ships sailing from Ayr harbour. Other freight involved the movement of steel and cars to Stranraer Harbour, supplying Roche of Dalry with material for the pharmaceutical plant, and finally, supplying goodness knows what to the munitions and ICI factories at Bogside and Stevenson. Later on saw the famous silver bullet trains coming to Irvine, but other than learning the road into the new plant at Irvine, my involvement in these trains was nil.

One of the most despised jobs at the depot, from a freight perspective, involved a double trip from Ayr Harbour to Knockshinnoch DP, up in the hills above New Cumnock. After booking on duty at 0505, following preparation, the 2 x Class 20s would be driven off the depot and taken to Ayr Harbour to collect the 32 HAA wagons for the job. If all had gone to plan thus far, the train would leave Falkland Yard between the 0545 and 0615 passenger trains. Arrival at Bank Junction and onto branch itself would be at around 0700, and a slow bimble would follow into Knockshinnoch, with proceedings coming to an end at 0730. If you were still feeling sleepy, the loading of the train would definitely wake you up. The empties were pushed uphill under the rapid loader, and then the loaded train came back down again. There was no room whatsoever for complacency, as by the time the last wagon was filled with a load of Ayrshire's finest, the leading Class 20 would be no more than twelve inches from the level crossing gates. There was no margin for error, and it was not a job for the faint-hearted, especially on a damp rail or misty morning.

Most crews would take a well-earned break at this point, as once you were back on the main line, then there was less opportunity to kill time. The reasons for this will become clearer later. Normally, we waited to come off the branch at Barassie, after the 0900 electric service from Glasgow had passed. This gave an arrival back in Falkland Yard of around 1000. The harbour pilot was waiting to take the train off you, and take it the short trip down the branch, to the discharge point. On paper, at least, we returned to Knockshinnoch immediately, for a second trip. In reality, this rarely happened, as wagons always seemed to be in short supply, and the later you arrived in Falkland, the less argument control had, to wait for the train to be emptied, and to take your own set back up. On the odd occasion this did happen, we took the train back up the hill, loaded it for a second time, and were then relieved by a fresh set of men at 1230. A local taxi firm then brought us home, allowing us to book off duty, a few minutes after 1400. Thankfully, the afternoon shift was not in my link. However, from memory, they took their train right into the harbour, before going light engine to Roche products at Dalry, to collect traffic which would go forwards to Carlisle on the 1840 Speedlink service. This was because there wouldn't be enough time for Knockshinnoch staff to load a third train.

We had several local trips. The first of the day booked on at 0500, and was more often than not formed of a Class 26 locomotive. The crew of driver, guard and second man took traffic from the overnight arrivals at Falkland to various locations in the area. This could include Roche products at Dalry, ICI at Stevenson, Bogside or Misk, Johnny Walker at Kilmarnock, or coal to Irvine. We always seemed busy, and scuttled backwards and forwards between the passenger services. It would be an exceptional shift if you were back on shed much before midday. We also had an afternoon shift doing likewise. On afternoons, you could go further afield, and find yourself at Mossend Yard with wagons requiring maintenance, or tripping defective DMUs to Glasgow Works, via the little-used City Union line in Glasgow. The Mossend trip involved a trip over the infamous Rutherglen and Carmyle line, towards Langloan Junction and Whifflet. It was not a place you'd want to break down at, especially with a trainload of something valuable, on your own, and with no direct communication with the signaller, other than through a long walk. In the junior link, this trip was often undertaken on a Friday, the worst nights of the week for neds. The train would be left in the downside at Mossend and the little engine scuttled off home light engine, as the traffic flow was normally inbound only.

Another big source of income for those of us in the junior links involved working local ballast trains around the area. Most of the work naturally fell at weekends, with the standard industry shifts of 2000 on Saturday and then 0300 and 1100 on Sundays, depending on the location of the work and the job itself. During my time at Ayr, I worked within possessions on the Glasgow road, G&SW north of Dumfries and also, on one occasion, Dalrymple Junction on the way to Girvan. The first and last shifts were usually the busy ones, as they involved setting the job up, and also the final shift, when the opposite applied, and the site was made ready for handing back to operational use. The middle shift, as at Inverness, could often see a driver sitting on the locomotive for the whole of the shift, without doing any work.

During the week, we would take spoil and other used material from weekend jobs to the tip at Shewalton. Wagons were tripped to/from the yard at Barassie or up yard at Irvine. As part of these operations, fresh ballast would also be collected from the local quarry at Hillhouse. This location off the Barassie to Kilmarnock line was accessed by climbing up off the main line, and over the A759 road into the hopper house. As part of the area's ballast programme, we crewed a single shifted pilot at Irvine Monday-Friday, and made up trains in the yard for weekend requirements. On a Friday, we returned the 08 locomotive to Ayr TMD for servicing, and would gallop along the main line at 15mph, trying to dodge faster trains between loops and sidings. I can't ever recall bringing the engine back to Irvine, and can only assume this was done sometime over the weekend by one of the other links of drivers. It's years since I last passed through Irvine. However, I'm led to believe that most of the yard is in now part of the inevitable town centre retail park, where once useful land is turned over to the relentless and puerile retail experience.

My link also worked on the back-shift harbour pilot at Ayr. The shift was 1300-2100 and with luck and some hard work, you could be finished and home indoors by 2000. The regular shunter down the harbour was a guy known to us all as 'Wee Andy' – a real character, and a man who loved a drink. However, this did not stop him putting in a solid shift, and he certainly wasn't afraid of hard work. We would bring the HAA wagons loaded with coal down from Falkland Yard, or collect them in the loop, if they had already been brought down by the train engine. Wagons were then split into batches of around eight and worked at 0.5mph over the discharge hopper. Andy would be working furiously, checking and closing doors after all the coal had fallen down onto the conveyer belt. From there it went into the hold of one of the ships waiting for a full cargo, to trip over the Irish Sea to Kilroot power station, near Carrickfergus. The empty wagons were taken back in the loop, and the next batch was taken down, to repeat the cycle all over again. Not the most glamorous of jobs, but something I hugely enjoyed. I loved being out of the limelight and away from the glare of officialdom. Andy was good company and had a wicked sense of humour. A day spent with him was very much a day well spent, even if it did end in a public house on Prestwick Road.

The people

Along with Andy, Ayr had several other characters on its books. We had a driver on restricted duties who had part of his leg missing. He always worked the same day-shift ballast job, and was known amongst his colleagues as 'Douglas Bader', of Dam-busting fame. The roster clerk was a man by the name of Craig Robertson. To me, he seemed to hate drivers with a vengeance. It was always a mystery to me why BR would give a job that involved getting drivers to do things above the call of duty to a man who hated us, but maybe it was just me he didn't like. He would go out of his way to claw back a few minutes' time off you, or decline a request for an exchange of duty, no matter how trivial. If you asked him a question, he would shrug his shoulders and walk away. He must have been a very bitter man, although I never did find out why. His attitude must have backfired on him at times: if a really big favour was needed, then it would be one of the foremen, such as Alex McClure, Bob Hastings or Andy Cooke who would call it in. Alex was by far the best man manager amongst the supervisors, and most of us would always do him a favour.

Our Traction Inspector and chief tormentor of young drivers was a man by the name of Eddie Carr. 'Big Eddie', as he was known, came from a railway family from Stranraer, and was at the time one of the youngest inspectors in the country. He was an OK chap and wouldn't really go out of his way to do you down. He liked to be respected and wouldn't take any lip. However, I can't ever remember crossing swords with him, and only remember him travelling in the cab with me on more than a couple of occasions.

The Glasgow Central-based traction inspectors were an entirely different kettle of fish. George Braun and his colleague were very old school, and almost expected young drivers to stand up and salute if they entered the driving cab. They took no prisoners. If you didn't have all your publications, or a collar and tie on a passenger train, then you would be on a charge, and up before the Train Crew Manager the following week.

I often ask myself why my driving career did not continue for longer than the 32 months that it did. Ayr certainly wasn't Inverness, but it wasn't a bad place to work, either. The work was varied, the wages reasonable, and I had the utmost respect for most of the people I worked with. The catalyst, if anything, was the first flushes of the break-up of the industry, ahead of a possible privatisation. Even in 1989, the depot and its work were being carved up into freight and passenger links, with the loss of the InterCity work to Stranraer and Carlisle to be replaced by the bland Class 156 sprinters. I could see a future for myself in the freight link, as my seniority would preclude me from passenger work. This really was the end of the railway I had joined, and the thought of losing many of my skills wasn't one that sat comfortably.

I was driving the midday DMU from Ayr to Girvan one day towards the end of 1988. Our TCM Alistair Smith came for a trip out with me. I recall he was having a bad day at the office and wished to 'disappear' for a few hours' thinking time. In the days before mobile phones, the best way to do this was in a driving cab. After exchanging pleasantries, along with getting an update on the progress of Alistair's restoration job on a recently acquired Morris Minor, we sat in silence, with Alistair obviously deep in thought. As we rattled through Kilkerran at 65mph, the opportunity presented itself for me to let the boss know how I was feeling about the job and its future prospects. Thankfully, as a former driver himself, Alistair was very understanding, and suggested that I nipped into his office later in the week, to discuss some possible options. He was true to his word, and when we sat down over a cup of coffee, he had several possible ways forwards to discuss. They were:

Apply to join the excellent British Railways management training scheme as an internal applicant. If I were successful, this would see me join with external graduates for an extensive two-year training programme. Providing the process had been taken seriously, at the end of this, a management appointment was guaranteed.

Apply for a junior management or supervisory role and if successful, work myself up through the ranks.

Go for the half-way house of becoming a Driver Instructor or panel TCS. This would mean that I didn't have to sever my ties with the driving grades completely, and was very much a try-before-you-buy arrangement.

It didn't take me many days to decide that option two was the one that I wished to pursue. I didn't feel academically ready to go toe-to-toe with graduates, nor did I want to stay as a driver and be a part-time manager. It felt as if it was time to move on, and that time was now. The first role I applied for was TCS at Motherwell. I was successful in getting an interview, but looking back, my chances of ever getting the job were nil. I was being tested out, and the grilling I was given by the panel, including Regional Chief Inspector Jimmy Alexander, really showed up my naivety, and how much learning was still needed. My next interview was for Traction Inspector Dundee, although the interview was held upstairs above Platform 4 in Perth. This time, Regional TCM Malcolm Knight joined Jimmy, and between them, they wiped the floor with me for a second time. On leaving the interview room, Jimmy asked me to wait outside the building for him. He followed me down a few minutes later and handed me a set of traction and train crew instructions, telling me to devour them cover to cover before coming in front of him again. This was duly done..A few weeks later, I saw a supervisory D-grade TCS role at Millerhill, and decided to try my luck for a third time. The interview was held out at Millerhill, a few weeks before Christmas. I was released from duty to attend, and given a pass to travel from Ayr to Edinburgh and told where to get the half-hourly staff minibus to take me from the Waverley and out to the yard itself. This time, my interview went very well. I was confident, articulate, and equipped myself very well. I didn't get the job, and subsequently found out a young driver from Millerhill was the successful applicant. However, I could tell it was only a matter of time, and as I travelled home on the 1530 push-pull service, my morale was high.

A few days later on 21 December, I booked on at 1630 and worked an additional Speedlink service to Carlisle, hoping to travel home passenger on the 2040 ex Carlisle. The train was a light one weightwise, and my Class 47 began to eat up the miles with consummate ease. Sadly, my train was to get no further than Dumfries. As I passed Maxwelltown Junction, the Dumfries distant was at caution and the night sky unusually bright. Without being told why, I received instructions from the signal man to leave my train in Dumfries yard and to return to Ayr light engine. It may have only been a Wednesday, but an early finish was always welcome. It was only when I got back to Ayr TMD that I found out about the sad and tragic events that were unfolding only a few miles from Dumfries. This was, of course, the destruction of flight 103 over the small town of Lockerbie. As I was bimbling up the Nith Valley with my small train, 270 innocent souls lost their lives after the New York bound jet was brought down by an act of terrorism 31,000 feet over southwest Scotland. Events such as this certainly put life in perspective. Christmas 1988 was a very subdued affair in the UK, and no doubt further afield.

January 1989 dawned grey and miserable, and was made worse by Manchester United thumping Liverpool 3-1 in front of 45,000 fans at Old Trafford. The match was bizarre, in that John Barnes put Liverpool in the lead on the 70-minute mark, but nine minutes later, Man U were 3-1 ahead, and the game was effectively over. We of course went on to win the FA Cup, after beating city rivals Everton 3-2 at Wembley.

On 12 January, I once again travelled through to Edinburgh for another interview. This time, it was in the Waverley itself, and for another Supervisory Grade D, but this time based at Haymarket. The job was mine to lose. I sensed this after the first few questions. The whole ambience was gentler and more relaxed. It was no great surprise when the final question they asked was about my availability to attend the methods of instruction course in Watford, in the first week in February. My career had been mapped out for me by these wise gentlemen. A few more years teaching rules, regulations and how to drive trains would make up for the limited amount of time I had actually been a driver. All this was confirmed to me in writing a few days later, and my countdown to a new career had begun.

At the time of my interview, my link was in the process of learning the route to Ravenstruther near Carstairs. A new opencast coal loading point was being built, and Ayr drivers were to haul most of the output to Ayr harbour. Every day, we travelled on the 0745 ex Ayr before walking down to the low-level station at the Central. Here, we boarded an empty Class 303 unit that had come from Yoker, before travelling to Carstairs via Rutherglen, and then, depending on the day of the week, to Newton, Motherwell and Lanark, or Newton, Hamilton, Motherwell, Holytown and Wishaw, or Uddingston, Bellshill, Holytown and Wishaw. This involved three weeks of route learning in total per driver. Even though I was leaving, never to see the site again except from passing trains, I was still expected to complete my training, before being passed out on the route by Traction Inspector John Shields. Not all of BR was efficient, and with things done on a strict seniority basis, it was very hard to make exceptions. Ironically, my final week as a driver was on the same shift as it started: 1600 Girvan, and ending with the 2115 ex Stranraer. On Saturday 18 February, as I walked away from my now silent DMU, it was very much an anti-climax. Without even a goodbye, I walked out of the gate at Ayr TMD, and I never looked back – well, not for a long time, at least.

NEVER GO BACK. AYR TMD IN 2016. NOW ALL GONE AND JUST ANOTHER RAILWAY GHOST.

Chapter 6 - Beginning Of The End

The move into a supervisory role was actually rather painless. My first of several visits to the impressive and imposing Grove House near Watford, was both educational and informative. The estate on which the house was built could trace its roots back to the 1400s, before it became the family home of the Earl of Clarendon, right through to the 1920s. The house took on a ministerial role during World War Two, after which the LMS railway used the building for numerous purposes, including training its managers and executives. This good practice was then continued by the British Transport Commission and, later still, British Railways Board. Sadly, the house fell into disrepair in the lead up to privatisation, so the visit in 1992 was to be my last. The week was made up of lectures, coursework and a very daunting presentation to others on the course. This was also filmed and then played back to me, to enable me to see what went well, and where improvements could be made. I kept a copy of the tape for many years, and I must admit I looked like a frightened rabbit in the headlights, as I stood in front of my peers and lecturers, to begin my talk on RETB signalling. Thankfully, I passed, and travelled home to Glasgow on the Thursday night with my Grove tie in my bag – everyone was given a Grove tie on their first visit. I knew my City and Guilds certificate which, would enable me to instruct and prepare course material, would be sent to me in a few weeks' time.

My first day back at Haymarket was on Monday 6 February 1989, nine years to the day since I walked into the depot as a raw recruit. It was cold and wet as I alighted from the 0800 push-pull ex Queen Street. As it was my first day in a salaried role, I felt it prudent to work to the book, and walked to the shed via the official walking route, down Haymarket Terrace and along Russell Road up to the shed itself. On such a wet morning, I can't claim it was a nice walk, but it was certainly a nostalgic one after all that had gone before, and the almost four-year gap since I finished MP12. The first thing I noticed was the fact that all the drivers had been moved to the Waverley since my last visit. The engineman's lobby was an eerie and empty place to be, given the noise and life it once contained.

I was, of course, familiar with the building, and several of the old faces remained, including Dick, Tam, Roy McCarthy and the guy I was replacing, Tom Philbin. After exchanging the usual pleasantries, I was given my first cup of gaffer's tea, as Tam called it. No more paper cups for me, as this one came in a china mug. Mind you, he did caveat it with, "bring your own bloody mug tomorrow, as you're no borrowing one of my best yins every day".

The first week was set aside for induction, with visits arranged to all the classes running at the time. This included MP12 rules, MP12 traction, train man training and finally, an HST conversion course. The visits were really only a sheep dip, and an insight into how each training subject was taught, as well as the different teaching styles of the instructors. If I had any grand ideas of the tasks that I would be given in my early career, they did not last for long. I had not been in the post for many weeks, when one day, Dick called me into his office to tell me he had the perfect job for me to cut my teeth on. For the next six weeks, I was to run two courses per day, each of three hours' duration, training drivers on the soon-to-be-introduced National Radio Network NRN system. The lesson plan required me to do an hour's theory, then attendees were given an opportunity to use the crude early generation simulator provided for the job. This Heath Robinson DIY simulator allowed drivers to make calls to me in the room, next door along, with me simulating incoming emergency broadcasts to the virtual cab next door. All good fun, and of course with a serious undertone, bearing in mind the advantages and disadvantages of this so-called instant communication. The morning session was for drivers based in the east at Millerhill, Edinburgh, Perth and Dundee, and the afternoon session for colleagues from the west at Eastfield, Polmadie and Carstairs. By the end of each week, my head was buzzing from going over the same material day after day. My six weeks 'Groundhog Day' of cutting my teeth soon ended, and I was in high hopes of something more exciting coming my way next. Naturally, Dick had another task to allow me to prove myself, before being fully unleashed into my new role. The "train man" concept, which was introduced by the British Railways Board the year before, now required all drivers, irrespective of age or experience, to undertake a biannual examination of rules and regulations. This was a huge challenge for drivers who had years of practical experience, but limited experience of theory. To cushion the blow, all those undertaking the assessment were given a coaching session by an instructor on the morning of the rules exam. It fell to me to run these morning sessions for another six weeks, prior to drivers from Millerhill and Edinburgh Waverley going before Traction Inspectors, Lou Gracie or Brain Panton in the afternoon. This was inspirational on Dick's part, as over the six weeks, I got to meet dozens of drivers in the Edinburgh area, and also build my confidence with senior men who were able, but perhaps not willing to adapt to change, or in some extreme cases, showed total apathy and disengagement towards anything new or different.

From May 1989, the basic traction for all new drivers from the non-electrified Scottish depots became the Class 150 Sprinter. All the years of Class 47 training, colouring in pipework and learning all about ROPs, SOPs and such like, was at an end. The future was *Sprinter*. As part of my training on these DMMUs, I was given the job of producing much of the new training notes for me and my colleagues to use in class. Therefore, my enthusiasm was now directed towards using the photocopier and writing acetates out by hand, with information provided by the engineering office downstairs for such an in-depth training course. The course consisted of modules on:

- Layout and design.

- Systems, fuel, oil, water and air.

- Electrical circuits.

- Preparation and disposal.

- Coupling and fault finding.

Each day's training was laid out with a recap of previous day, an introduction to what would be covered today, a review of the day, and finally, an insight into the next day. I later learned this was called, "tell them what you are going to tell them", "tell them" and finally "tell them what you have told them". Simples, really!

Before long, I had a pile of notes, view foils and photographs for Dick and Roy to endorse and sign off. After a few changes and improvements from the more experienced men, they were ready to be used in earnest on the first group of trainee drivers. I asked Dick who I should pass the material over to, as I knew the first course was booked for a couple of weeks' time. "You keep them, son," he said. "You wrote it, so you can deliver it. I will be watching you all the way, so no pressure." At long last, my chance to prove myself on the big stage of group classroom teaching had arrived. A five-week class all on my own. I put on the instructor's blue dustcoat and did my utmost to ensure my eight trainees had the best possible experience. I was on cloud nine.

So, after the May Bank Holiday, we kicked off the course, and my real life as a Traction Instructor began. I admit to feeling very nervous as I stood in front of 'my laddies', for the first time and gave them an overview of all that lay ahead. Sadly, the names of the trainees have been lost in the mists of time, but they would have been a mix from Edinburgh, Perth and possibly Dundee or Stirling, as drivers from the West of Scotland were trained in Rutherglen. I know no Inverness drivers were involved, as I would have remembered meeting my old mates. Training Inverness drivers would need to wait for a later day. After cutting my teeth on my first driver training course, I went on to take a further traction course and two full rules courses, as part of the quest to keep newly qualified drivers coming on stream, to match the huge retirement and resettlement profile of the time.

In between delivering training courses, I was given a couple of weeks tuition on HSTs, which was made up of a week in the classroom and then a week out on the road, driving between Edinburgh and Newcastle. Although as I still lived in Ayr, I used to get some extra cab experience by joining the 0800 Glasgow QS to London Kings Cross, and travelling through to Edinburgh to meet my instructor for a drive to Newcastle with the 0930, and home with the down *Flying Scotsman*. I must admit that I struggled with the high-speed braking on these units. It was a far cry from driving them at 75-80mph over the Highland Line. I was constantly accused of braking early and light, and as a result, dropping time. In mild desperation, my tutor suggested that I sit in the right-hand seat and let the expert show me how it was done. So off we charged into the Northumberland countryside, with the expert now at the controls. The braking for the 75mph through Alnmouth was severe, and the power came on hard for the climb of Longhoughton bank. We flashed through Chathill with the speedo hovering at around 120mph, before charging along the racing stretch past Belford and Crag Mill. To cut a long story short, this so-called expert messed up the braking for a red signal at Scremerston, and as I was being given a demonstration of precision 'top link' driving, everything was left a tad late. We passed over the AWS magnet for the red at 30mph with the emergency brake applied. Somehow, we came to a shuddering halt with the nose of the HST perfectly aligned with the signal post telephone. The 'expert' was ashen-faced, and it was only just dawning on him how close we had come to a 'passing the signal at danger' (SPAD) event. There was no harm done and nothing ever got reported or spoken about, from that day to writing these words. Of course, the name shall never be revealed, out of respect to my former colleague. Not much else was said as we ran the remainder of the 60-odd miles to Edinburgh in near silence. On the Friday, it was the usual grilling from Senior Traction Inspector Lou Gracie, involving both theory and practical demonstrations of my knowledge. We started in the Waverley and then transferred over to Craigentinny for access to a power car. I remember Lou had a new Citroen car, and I was totally in awe of how the suspension inflated and deflated when the engine was started. We also stopped in Leith to buy filled rolls for lunch somewhere on Easter Road. His treat, so thanks once again for that. By 1600 we were done, and I could now add HST power cars and Mark 3 coaches to my growing list of traction knowledge.

With each passing month, my confidence grew. Within a year, I could stand in front of my class and teach large sections of the course material from memory. The book itself was only being needed to resolve clarification questions, or to show trainees how the rules in different parts of the book knitted together, to give the overall safety umbrella to which we all needed to work. While it was not my reason for teaching in this front-of-desk style, I could tell it impressed trainees that this former driver could stand in front of them and quote large sections of the rules and regulations from memory. In fact, on more than one occasion, one of the trainees would pull me to the side at lunch or break time to say that one day, when their driving career was over, they hoped it would be them teaching new members of staff the ropes. Even Dick was mildly impressed, as when he sat in on my classes to review progress, he always offered kind words of support, along with the odd nugget of things which could be done better, no doubt to keep my feet firmly on the ground.

Life was good. I was a married man, now living in Falkirk with less than an hour's commute door to door, and I had every weekend off. I was growing into my role, and had the respect of my colleagues, superiors and trainees. The only dark cloud on an otherwise bright horizon was how poorly paid we were, considering all the knowledge and responsibility the role carried. My take-home pay was under £200 per week. My wife, who worked in insurance, earned half this again. This gave us a combined monthly income of £1,217. With a mortgage and general household bills to pay, and the desire to do all the usual things a young couple may want to enjoy, the situation wasn't sustainable long term. We couldn't even afford to run a car. With town centre living, this wasn't a huge issue, but it would be, if we decided to start a family or live in more rural surroundings.

Some brief respite came when Dick informed me that I was one of the instructors chosen to do out-based training of the 156 Sprinter DMU, at my former home depot of Inverness. To fit training into a week's theory, we would travel up on Sunday evening, ready for a 0900 start on Monday. After lodging all week, we would travel home on the 1230 ex Inverness on Fridays. Six hours of Sunday pay for travelling up, and four hours of overtime for travelling home all made a difference to the bottom line. I also got to enjoy spending time with my former colleagues, along with cycling and walking in the area some evenings, plus, of course, the odd pint or two with my old pals.

The lodgings we were billeted in was a small, cosy and well-run family guest house in Tomnahurich Street, ironically not far from my old home in May Court. More often than not, I would allow the trainees to leave at 1500, hours before spending an hour preparing any photocopied training material needed for the next day. This would allow me to leave the depot at 1600 and enjoy a coffee on one of the riverside hotels, and easily get back to my lodgings for the evening meal at 1700. This left enough time for an evening stroll round the city centre, along the Ness banks or even a bike ride further afield, along the towpath to Dochgarroch on the Caledonian Canal. However, the training was intense, because the lines north and west were severed by the collapsed Ness viaduct. The pressure was on to get enough numbers of Inverness staff trained, to allow some 156 units to be deployed north of the block, for the high summer working. I believe ultimately a small number of 156 units were sent to Invergordon by road, to allow a similar number of 37s to be brought south, and sent to new homes in the various freight pools, including St Blazey in Cornwall. I spent six consecutive weeks living my life in this fashion, but like all good things, by the end of June, it came to an end. It was back to flat week's wages, and days locked in the classroom at Haymarket. It was my wife who first suggested that it was time for me to look for a better-paid job. A traction inspector role anywhere within Scotland was the obvious move, and fortuitously, Jock Bruce up in Inverness decided to retire early. The opportunity was about to knock.

I really wanted the job, and put in a huge amount of time and effort to get ready for interview, should I be granted one. The thought of returning to Inverness and settling down for the long haul in such an idyllic part of the world was worth the effort. Eventually the call to interview came, with the location of the grilling being Perth. The panel was made up of Malcolm Knight, Traction and Train Crew Manager for Scotland, along with his Chief Inspector, my old nemesis, Jimmy Alexander. I had the interview of my life. I breezed every question and felt as if I had strong motivation for wishing to return to the Highlands. I left the interview on cloud nine, and felt it was only a matter of time before the call came..Perhaps a little prematurely, we even began to look at houses and jobs in the Highlands for my wife, Karen. Thankfully, we didn't actually commit to anything, as about a week later, Dick asked me to stop back at the end of the working day for a chat. This sounded ominous, and indeed it was. Dick told me that while I had acquitted myself well at interview, I wasn't being offered the job. It was felt I was still close to my former mates in Inverness, and this had been witnessed by persons unspecified during my time training 156s. This closeness was a potential conflict of interests, and therefore the job had been offered to someone with no previous ties at the depot. To say that I was disappointed was an understatement. From my perspective the 156 training had been done by the book, in an environment that was both professional and cordial. I purposely avoided going for after-work drinks with the men, other than a few final night beers with Graham Pirie, on my last evening in town. The whole saga felt like a stitch-up, and it was probably my first experience of the best man not always getting the job. If your face – and indeed beard – fitted, the job was yours, but not necessarily on merit. This wasn't in the script, and right there and then, I knew my time in Scotland was at an end. Even after a few days sleeping on things, my view didn't change. The beginning of the end of this chapter of my life was set in motion.

Once again, opportunity was about to knock as the Train Crew Leader concept was being rolled out on the Eastern Region, and new posts were being created at just about every location. Applications were made for Newcastle, Leeds and a place that I had never heard of before, called Blyth Cambois, in that order of preference. I was given interviews for all three, and was rejected for Leeds, but offered both Newcastle and Blyth. Thankfully, I was never associated with the despised 'Hitler Youth' at Leeds, not that it would have been my style of leadership, so the badge was never mine to wear. Terry Hutton and Geoff Mansell took the Newcastle interview, and Jimmy Richardson and Geoff the Blyth interview. Newcastle was definitely the better gig, with numerous tractions, including the HST and the imminent arrival of the Class 91, London to Edinburgh and Leeds route knowledge, and a great bunch of colleagues to work with. Blyth on the other hand offered only coal and more coal, and an endless diet of Class 56 locomotives. On the plus side, housing was cheap in that part of Northumberland, and the job was mine to make whatever I wanted of it. Jimmy Richardson really came across as wanting me to join him, to the extent of putting my wife and me up in a hotel for a weekend, to allow her to take a good look around. Despite my head saying Newcastle, my heart won the day, and it was an easy decision to accept Jimmy's kind offer of a job at Blyth. This decision set me off on a path that would take me through the rest of my career. With only one exception, Blyth was without a shadow of a doubt the best place I have ever worked at. Great depot, great people and a real can-do culture.

My final day as a Haymarket man was on 16 February, just a year since I first left the security of the footplate. I had a small leaving lunch with my former colleagues, and said my fond farewells to a great bunch of guys. I was sorry to be leaving, but everyone understood my motivation for doing so, and we promised to keep in touch. I had already secured lodgings in Morpeth. As I was still without a car, I would need to rely on lifts and public transport for a few weeks of my new adventure.

On Monday 19th, I arrived at the windswept depot by the sea for the very first time. A harsh wind blew in off the sea, and it felt more like Siberia than England. Blyth Cambois was an out-base of the newly formed Area Manager's office at Sunderland. We had a small stud of Toton class 56s, a two-road shed and fuelling facilities, an Area Operations Centre (AOC) and a small but dedicated team of fitters and drivers. All this was overseen by an MS1 General Manager by the name of Paul Atack.

The main reason for the creation of my role was to support the experienced Traction Inspector Bob Blackburn, who had been at the depot for many years. I also had to help set up the new driver training facilities needed for the large influx of new drivers over the coming years, further compounded by the imminent demise of the regional training facilities in Doncaster, Leeds and Newcastle. The Organising for Quality (OFQ) initiative was in full swing, and the British Railways regions as we knew them would be abolished by 1992.

We had a classroom, but not much else. I was given a budget by Jimmy Richardson, and told in no uncertain terms that we needed to be open for business by April. My counterpart, Nigel Stacy in Sunderland, was doing likewise, albeit on a slightly smaller scale, as most of the training was to be delivered at the Blyth end. Nigel and I worked well together as a team, and forged a lifelong friendship which has continued on/off right to the present day. While Nigel and I were busy spending Trainload Freight's money, along with writing training notes and producing handouts, Bob Blackburn and his Sunderland-based opposite number, Ernie Hewitson, kept the day job running. Nigel was a former South Dock driver, so was able to train me on the superb Class 56s, before Ernie passed me out as a competent driver, thus giving me my 12th traction on my ever-increasing traction card.

Once again, in the same style as Haymarket, I was given an easier job to cut my teeth on. From 16 to 21 October, I was to deliver a 'guard to driver's assistant' course. The new line of promotion was described by some as the 'back to front stunts'. I found the trainee, George Wilkinson, to be engaged and engaging, although it was strange to run a weeklong course 1-to-1.

Somehow, I was often given the task of assessing the driver on 6S56, the West Blyth to Millerhill tanks, on a Friday morning. The train left West Blyth at around 0710, with an arrival in Millerhill just before 1000. This was a one-way job for us, so a blind eye was always turned to me traveling home to Falkirk to complete the paperwork, and get the weekend started early. During the first few months based at Blyth, I enjoyed trips to Millerhill with **37099, 37092, 37097** and **37049.**

Some excellent drivers came out of our small training facility. Even now, the names trip off the tongue easily. Brian and Nigel Batch, Neil Alcock, Brian Wynn and Ronnie Fowler, to name but a few.

Jimmy Richardson was pretty hands-off when it came to things we four were involved in. This was unsurprising, as he was a very busy man, with customers, suppliers, engineers, signallers and a whole bunch of other stuff, all eating into his working day. The area manager, Cathleen Gregory, was equally busy. Other than bumping into her on the odd occasion, we were pretty much self-managed, which suited me and my colleagues just fine.

For the first few months, I lodged in Morpeth Sunday to Thursday, and then travelled home to Falkirk at weekends. This was not ideal, and not sustainable in the long term. I had gone from poorly paid but comfortable, to reasonably well paid, but living out of a suitcase. This wouldn't be the last time in my career that I lived my life in such a way. Respite finally came when we sold our flat in Falkirk and bought a former mining cottage in the small village of Pegswood. Mrs MacLennan, who worked in insurance at the time, managed to secure a transfer to the Newcastle branch of the company she worked for, so life was about to return to a degree of stability.

In between setting-up training facilities and such, both Nigel and I were summoned to York to meet and be offered wise counsel by Regional Chief Traction Inspector Geoff Mansell. We met him in the very grandiose surroundings of the ER HQ, at Hudson House. Geoff made a point of seeing all his newly-appointed inspectors. He took great care to instil in us exactly what he expected of us, and in turn, what we could expect of him. I can categorically state that rules were not a guide, nor was the speed of a train anything other than to be adhered to. A strict adherence to both was now very much in order. Geoff came across as the total professional railway man, in every respect. He reminded me greatly of Lou Gracie, as both seemed the perfect role model for young, ambitious managers such as me. After finishing formalities with 'The Chief', Nigel took us to the staff association club for a spot of lunch, and then the first available HST back to Newcastle.

I hadn't been at the depot for many months when I had my first encounters with two of the north east's more infamous drivers. Sid Triggs at South Dock and Stan Oram at Blyth were old school, and had very little, if any, respect for authority, especially young inspectors in a suit and tie. Sid referred to me as the "whipping boy", and as for Stan, we just never hit it off whatsoever, and my views of him are best kept private. Ironically, after he retired, a few months later, I inherited his bardic lamp, and for the rest of my time at Blyth, enjoyed using a hand lamp stencilled as the "property of Stan Oram".

On reflection, I don't really resent Stan or Sid's behaviour. Both men had joined the railway just after World War Two, and were no doubt struggling with the pace of change, as I am, after 40 years of my own service to the industry.

In between stints in the classroom, I began to build up a route card, to reflect the depot's core workload. Blyth to Ashington, Butterwell and Widdrington came first, to be followed by some further afield destinations such as Wardley, Tyne Dock and Tyne Yard. The depot had booked work to Millerhill with the loaded Alcan tanks from North Blyth to Fort William, and also to York, with the Lynemouth to Ellesmere Port coal containers. Time prevented me from ever learning these routes properly, but I did achieve enough knowledge to allow me to undertake some of the driving, when carrying out assessments.

Our Millerhill job was an early one. We booked on before 0500 to prepare a train load metals sector Class 37, before running light to North Blyth to collect our train. We departed just before 0600, running via Bedlington Furnace Way (ERRT) Morpeth North Junction, and then onto the ECML. Arriving in Millerhill at around 0950, we disposed of the engine, before catching the staff bus into Edinburgh. If the day had gone to plan, we arrived on an HST in Newcastle around lunchtime, before a taxi from Newcastle back to Blyth.

The York turn was slightly more sociable, and would see us book on duty just before 0700. After preparing our Class 56, we ran light to Lynemouth, to collect our smart train of yellow box wagons. Departure with 6M21 would be at 0750, running via the Blyth and Tyne, Newcastle and then straight up the ECML, albeit on the slow lines from Northallerton. At Skelton Junction, we continued onto the slow lines past York Works, before finally surrendering our 56 to the forwards driver at Holgate Bridge relieving point. We walked the short distance to the station, before another HST ride back to Newcastle and the obligatory taxi to Cambois. Occasionally, though, things could go wrong. On 4 January 1991, we failed at Lynemouth, with a brake defect on **56122**. A replacement loco **56127** was dispatched from Blyth, although we left for York around 120 minutes late.

I enjoyed several trips on this job, with some excellent drivers, including Dave Armstrong, Bob (Bomber) Harris and Mark Conroy. The actual assessment was almost a formality, such was the high calibre of these chaps, not to mention the pride they held for the job they undertook, and the depot they represented.

Both of the above jobs were the nearest we ever got to the roaring main at Blyth. All the reaming turns were round the North East, hauling 36 full or empty HAA hoppers, or, as I got to know them later, at Margam buckets. Most of the other trip working involved going round the local loading points, and tipping it in Blyth power station. My own favourite trip, and one of the best to do assessments on, was the trip to Widdrington. The short trip involved yard working semaphore signalling, and a trip along the ECML, before arriving in the exchange sidings. After splitting the train, we then descended the brutal incline down to the disposal point of the same name. The first portion was loaded with black gold, and hauled, slipping and sliding, back up the hill, with the 56 screaming its head off, and using more sand than could be imagined. After catching our breath, the next 18 would be taken down, and the whole exercise repeated. Finally, once the train was put back together, and all the paperwork completed, we retraced our steps to either the power station, or further afield, if the coal was heading to one of the Yorkshire power stations.

56108 DEPARTS YORK ON 31/8/92 AFTER A CREW CHANGE WITH A LOAD OF BLACK GOLD HEADING FOR YORKSHIRE

56131 AND A LOAD EX MELKRIDGE SEEN HERE NEAR HAYDEN BRIDGE.

THE GREATEST PASSENGER TRAINS EVER BUILT AND ANOTHER TIMELESS SCENE AT YORK

A STARK REMINDER OF WINTERS PAST. THIS TIME ON THE WHL IN FEBRUARY 1984 WHERE MY OLD PAL GRAHAM MAXTONE CLAIMS IT WAS EVEN COLDER THAN UP NORTH.

SUNDERLAND SOUTH DOCK. HOME DEPOT OF THE SOMETIMES MILITANT 'DOCKERS'

56107 HEADS WITH 36 EMPTY HAA'S FOR FILLING IN THIS UNDATED SHOT

In November 1989, we began to operate a daily route-learning locomotive to Haltwhistle, ready for the opening of Plenmellor, or Melkridge, to railway men). Drivers who came up with me that first week included Kevin Paxton, Paul Dunn, Alan Summers, Paul Emmington and Ronnie Scott, to name but a few. One of my last tasks, prior to a final stint in the classroom at this wonderful little depot, involved the method of working testing for the now-closed open-cast mine at Plenmeller, near Haltwhistle. This site, which was situated on Plenmeller Common, had suffered some fierce local opposition during its planning stage, and took far longer than first envisaged to build. The site was finally completed in late summer of 1990. Lots of testing was required before the formal opening on 19 September. The first trip we made was a dry run. **56133**, John Tuck and I collected 22 POA wagons from Ryhope Grange near Sunderland. We left at 0222 in the morning and arrived up at location just before 0400. We ran straight through to test the run round arrangements at Haltwhistle, before departing back to Blyth for 0630, out of the way of the morning passenger services. The following week, driver Martin Rodgers and I were given the task of working a fully loaded test train. We set off from Blyth at 1600 with **56116** and a rake of HAAs up to the site, to test the rapid loader, weighbridge and signalling. We then loaded for Haltwhistle at 1845, before dropping the train down at TCFD, outside Newcastle. Then it was light back to Blyth, and off duty at 2200. This test was to secure the all-important tick in the box, to say the site was ready to use, although I left before the place really got going to its capacity.

The amount of coal we shifted for the customer was phenomenal. Often, two or three trains were waiting to enter the power station at Blyth, and get a slot under the discharge hopper. Tyne Dock was the same, and often you could wait an hour or more at Green Lane for a slot onto the dock. It was all impressive stuff and demonstrated BR at its very best. Trains were booked crew relief in the power station, before setting off for another ten hours on the road.

However, this wasn't to last, as the times, they keep a-changing. The boom in coal slowed. The Durham coal fields in particular got decimated, and it didn't take a genius to work out that the writing was on the wall..As a result of the reduced tonnages of coal, the West Blyth to Millerhill went over to Class 56 haulage in 1990. As an example, we had a double-headed run with **56030/56082** on 20 August, before bringing our own **56118** back to Blyth light engine.

Bob first sowed the seed that a move away to a location not wholly dependent on coal could be in my best long-term interest. Dawdon and Murton had gone, Easington and Seaham, along with Westoe, were all down for closure, and even Wearmouth was soon to follow.

My final turn as a Blyth Traction Inspector was on Friday 22 February 1991. I did an afternoon trip with my old friend Brian Batch and **56127**, and after, we arrived back on the reception road at the power station, I said my goodbyes and walked away with a new life in the Rhondda Valley awaiting..

APPENDIX A - From Moray Firth To Atlantic Wild

We're about to climb into the warm and welcoming cab of a Class 26/1 locomotive, at the business end of the 0655 passenger and mail train from Inverness to the Kyle of Lochalsh. It's February 1981, and a hard, penetrating frost has the Highland capital in its icy grasp.

The steady tick-over beat of the idling locomotive provides an almost hypnotic lullaby as the sound reverberates off the surrounding buildings. The first warm fingers of heat are forcing its way through the three-coach train, and the hiss of escaping steam from the numerous nooks and crannies add to the unmistakable feel of a different way of doing things.

A quick look is taken at the front of the locomotive, and we note the pin-prick dots of light from the marker discs over each buffer. The twin car-type main headlights are not fitted to this particular class member, and even if they were, they are switched off until passing under the Longman Road bridge, a few seconds after departure. This is to avoid dazzling the driver of the resident Class 08, who is busy collecting the day coaches and sleeping cars from the internal overnight in Platform 6, and tripping them the short distance to the carriage servicing sheds.

We climb aboard, and are immediately struck by the warmth of the footplate, as this type of locomotive has some of the best cab heaters on British Railways. The wall of heat greeting us is testament to the claim that no better machine has ever existed, in respect of performance and creature comforts, for the routes north and west of Inverness.

As we are in Number 2 cab, this places the small but efficient stones vapour steam heating generator directly behind us. We can hear the hum of the water pump, and the intermittent roar of the burner and its associated smells, as steam pressure is built up to the maximum of 40psi throughout the whole length of the short train.

Ten minutes before departure, the guard arrives with information on the train itself. Three vehicles for 105 tons, passengers aboard for the request stops at Loch Luichart and Duncraig. Any others will be advised to the crew, either by hand signal from the guard's van or from passengers themselves, who may wish to join at any of the remaining halts. Finally, and all importantly, a small bundle of newspapers are given to us. These are for the signal men at Garve, Achnasheen, Strathcarron and Kyle, with the remainder for the footplate mess room at Kyle. Stations before Dingwall will be taken care of by the crew of the 0615 to Wick.

At around 0653, the Rose Street signaller arrives with the single line token for the very short 1.5 mile section to Clachnaharry. With the starting signal already cleared, lift off was imminent. At exactly 0655, the tip from the guard was given, and the power handle of the little engine nudged gently open to get its train underway. As we straightened out past the site of the harbour branch, the large brass handle was fully opened, and the timeless Sulzer rasp echoed out over the empty streets and frost-covered roof tops. Speed got no higher than 40mph, as after passing 'Clach Park', the home of Clachnacudden Football Club, the brakes came on for the 8mph restriction over the canal bridge ahead.

The Davis and Metcalfe brake valve on a Class 26 was very noisy, and filled our ears with a loud woooooshing sound, making speech impossible, as the vacuum in the train pipe was destroyed and the train speed reduced. The bridge over the Caledonian Canal was built by the Highland Railway Company in 1862, and passing over it made a sound that made you think that despite the train only traveling at 8mph, it was about to collapse underneath you.

The first token exchange was made successfully, and we now had permission to proceed to Lentran and the next crossing point. As soon as the locomotive had passed the Clachnaharry Inn, the power came on hard for the 1:150 climb to Bunchrew. Running alongside the deserted A9 road, we all discussed why an old fishing boat had been moored at the mouth of the canal. Apparently, it had been there for most of the year and unbeknown to us, would remain at anchor for the next 18 months, before mysteriously disappearing, destination unknown. The tide was high, and the first fingers of daylight were spreading onto the sea and Black Isle, as numerous sea birds swooped and wheeled in search of breakfast. Bunchrew Automatic Open Level Crossing carried a 25mph speed limit, so the brakes went on as we observed the crossing lights operating, and the white proving light illuminate to allow the driver authority to proceed. As it was after 0700 (rule book restrictions on horn use between 2300-0700), the driver was allowed to give a long blast on the horn, as an additional warning to road users of the imminent arrival of 200 tons of moving metal. Another burst of power had us moving along at 60mph, before a further slowing to 10mph for the exchange of tokens with the signalman at Lentran.

Following a cold blast as the cab window slid open, the heavy leather pouch really slammed against the outside door, before being hauled aboard for the run to the first stop at Muir of Ord. The Sulzer snarl was again unleashed into the morning air, as we scampered along one of the faster sections, with 70mph being attained either side of the bridge over the river, and passed the site of the former station at Beauly, closed in 1960 and of course opened in 2002, as Britain's most expensive platform, metre per metre. After running uphill and past the golf course and the malting siding, we glided to a halt in the reopened station at the Muir of Ord, a little after 20 minutes since leaving Inverness. No passengers boarded or alighted, but some mail bags and newspapers were off-loaded to make the stop worthwhile. The aroma of baking pies and bread from the nearby Forbes bakery awoke our taste buds, and reminded everyone that breakfast in Kyle was still several hours away. After another exchange of tokens at the signal box adjacent to the former junction for the Fortrose branch, it was downhill at 70mph through dense woodland, before once again meeting the A9 near Conon Mains farm. Another river crossing and former station site, this time at Conon Bridge, quickly followed, although we had to slow to 40mph for the speed restricted bridge over the salmon-rich river.

With 19 miles covered and some brisk station work completed at Dingwall (or Inverpeffer, as it was originally known) we were now about to enter the Kyle line proper, as we branched away from the Far North line, just after leaving the station at Dingwall North. With another token on board, this time for the 12-mile run to Garve, the Road to the Isles was ours. It was amazing to think that less than ten years earlier, the route had still been under the threat of closure, and it was only through vigorous campaigning that the line was kept open, with final confirmation of the line's future coming on 19 August 1974. We bimbled over a couple of open crossings at Dingwall, numbers 1 & 2 thus keeping the speed down to 20mph, before running at 40mph along the valley floor to Fodderty, with the hills of the Cats Back and Knockfarrel towering above us. We slowed for the 20mph bridge over the A834 along with the River Peffrey, as we passed the site of the former junction for the short Strathpeffer branch, closed in 1951.

We were now on the testing climb to the Raven's Rock, and for the first time since leaving Inverness, as we climbed away from the valley floor, it felt as if our small engine was fighting a losing battle with gravity, as the 1:50 climb to the 460 foot summit bit hard. With the hills of the Heights of Fodderty and

Achterneed closing in on the right, the reverberating sound of a hard-working engine became all-consuming, as the Type 2 did all that was asked of it. The crossing at the site of Achterneed station had a severe speed restriction, due to road users having restricted view of approaching trains. On such a fierce gradient, no brake application was needed, and by an early closing of the power handle, speed reduced nicely to the line's limit of 10mph. Another good tooting and parping on the locomotive's horn was undertaken, before another frenzied burst of power took us into the thick woodlands and the uninhabited ravine, ever nearer the line's summit a few miles ahead.

The Raven's Rock is a huge slab of granite which at some point in the 1800s had a single-track rail line blasted through the middle of it, no doubt mostly by hand, by our Victorian forefathers. The rock is visible from many miles in every direction, but due to its lack of road access, is rarely visited by man. The next six miles are all downhill, and we were advised to look out for wild cats and red deer, both of which could be found in the dense forests surrounding the area. We rocked and rolled downhill at 45mph, passing the remote cottage at Rogie before joining up with the A835 road along the shores of Loch Garve, and onwards towards the village of the same name. Despite its size, Garve was always busy, as it served as a railhead for large areas of the west coast, out towards Ullapool and several of the islands, including Lewis and Harris, which were reached by steamer from Ullapool. The train sat patiently for many minutes as several bags of mail, parcels and newspapers were off-loaded into mail vans and the post bus, for onward transit into even more remote communities. After what seemed like an age, and with the Garve to Achnasheen token safely on board, we were away again. The 1:50 climb began right at the end of the platform, and went on relentlessly for over two miles to the 429 foot summit of Corriemuille. The Munro, Ben Wyvis, sat proudly off to the right, its 3,250-foot summit lost in the morning mist, and the smaller Cnoc na h-Iolaire likewise to our left. With the sliding window open, the loco's exhaust snarl bounced off the trees and rocks either side of us, as the reliable engine dug in for the climb. The cab was filled with fresh clean mountain air, with a slight hint of moss and pine from the numerous forestry plantations in the area. It was just what we needed after such an early start, to help revitalise and reinvigorate the sleepy heads up front.

We crested Corriemuille at 30mph before plunging down the other side, as we twisted this way and that, through dense patches of silver birch, and towards the first encounter with Loch Luichart. When the valley was flooded as part of one of the 1960s hydroelectric schemes, the whole railway had to be moved to a new alignment, including the building of a new railway station. Water is fed by gravity from Loch Glascarnoch, 826 feet up in the hills, to drive the giant turbines, and help generate around 30MW of hydroelectricity. The old alignment is under about 15 feet of water, but puts in an occasional appearance in times, such as the summer drought of 1976. Today, we had a passenger to drop off and a couple to collect at the small, out-of-the-way hamlet, before powering out of the station and rumbling over the iron bridge at the west end of the loch. Another short, punchy climb followed, with the little engine snarling its way ever west, and across the peat moors in the shadow of Sgurr Mor, then across the next water course at Loch a Chuillin, and through a further hamlet, this time at Achnanalt. After passing through the station at 20mph, with no custom whatsoever, we galloped across the flat lands towards Achnasheen. With the River Bran and A832 all fighting for space in the pass, we were never far from river or road, as we bucked and swayed at 50mph, racing the few cars out and about at this time of day. On the approach to Achnasheen, we could see the first train of the day east, waiting patiently for our arrival. Its ubiquitous Class 26 idled away as it shrouded the red post van from Kinlochewe in milky white steam, awaiting the arrival of the mails and sundries from our rapidly emptying brake van. With precision-braking the van from the train, we brought to a halt opposite the post van and, no doubt contrary to all rules and regulations, the mail was thrown out of the off side of the train and into the waiting arms of the postie, who was standing track side at the end of the platform ramp.

The number of the eastbound 26 was lost as train crew exchanged waves, and a few out-of-season tourists or rail fans pointed their expensive cameras at the little locomotive. The single line token was ready and waiting for the onwards trip to Strathcarron, and so the eastbound train would depart second, as its token for Garve had to be put back through the machine by the temporary hard-working signaller, whose rush hour would be over by 0830.

THE POSTMAN AND HIS DOG COLLECT THE MAILS AT STROME FROM THE GUARD OF THE FIRST TRAIN WEST ON 31/10/73

A BUSY KYLE IN THE SUMMER OF 1982. JUST HOW I REMEMBER THE PLACE. 26035 WAITS TO HEAD HOME AT 1710

A SPLENDID LOOKING 37261 IS SEEN AT KYLE READY TO RETURN HOME AT 1710.

With its fuel and boiler water tank now emptying, the little locomotive took on a gentle rock as it waited to be unleashed on the climb to the line's summit at the Luib, the water shed of the River Bran and River Carron, both of which rise in the vicinity of Loch Scaven, with the Bran flowing east and ultimately to the North sea, and the Carron west to the Atlantic. As we attacked the climb with a noisy gusto, we could see the snowline of the mountains would almost be at rail level, before the 646-foot summit was reached. This was exactly what we had come to see, steam heat, snow and some of the most stunning scenery this world has to offer any rail traveller. The summit was taken at a rather nippy 40mph, before another downhill plunge through Glen Carron to the sea. We switched left, right, left again, up a short hump, before passing another deserted request stop at Achnashellach. This former private station, built for Viscount Hill, is more popular in the summer months, with hill walkers using it as the entry/exit point for the Torridon hills to the north. The distant signal for the level crossing gates at Balmacara on the shores of Loch Dughail was at caution, making us crawl up to the gates, only to find they were closed to road users, and the crossing keeper sheepishly exhibiting a green hand signal. After giving the said keeper some abuse on the high tone of the Type 2's horn, we were off again, and hit the highest speed since leaving Dingwall, with the train briefly touching 55mph on the long straight before Strathcarron and the final call of any significant importance before Kyle. Another pile of mailbags appeared on the platform, as the mails for the Applecross peninsula came off here, as did some boxes of food and such-like for the local village shop. With no more passing loops ahead, we took possession of the token for Kyle, and one of the most iconic rail journeys in the world along the shores of Loch Carron.

With the line speed from Strathcarron west no more than 35mph, and much of it 25mph, the few passengers were certainly getting their money's worth. We headed through Attadale, the avalanche shelter by the loch, and then onwards to Stromeferry (no ferry at Strome) to the next stop at the small station, serving the girls' boarding school at Duncraig. After departing the tiny platform at the base of the rock with the castle on top, we climbed round Plockton harbour and into the station of this small village. During the brief stop, the steam heating boiler was switched off, as this would allow any residual steam to be purged out of the system before the locomotive was uncoupled from the train at its destination. The little engine departed Plockton with its customary racket, and no doubt rattled a few windows in the row of bungalows just beyond the end of the platform, as once again we headed into open countryside and into one of the most expensive pieces of railway ever built in the UK, at £20,000 per mile, or almost £3,000,000 at today's prices.

The line was literally blasted out of solid rock, as 1,000s of tons of dynamite were brought in to open up the road to Kyle. In fact, the final ten miles took almost four years to complete. The first through-train from Inverness to Kyle ran on 2 November 1897, and was driven by driver John MacPherson of Inverness depot. The line side from here on in was thick with rhododendron bushes, We rounded Durnish bay, and in doing so, got our first glimpse of the inner sound, with the islands of Skye, Scalpay, Longay, Pabay and Raasay beyond, their mountain peaks hidden in the clouds. We picked up a couple of locals at Durnish, no doubt heading to Kyle for the weekly shop. A final burst of power took us past Erbusaig and Badicaul and to the final destination of Kyle of Lochalsh. After surrendering the single line token, and of course the last newspaper to the signal man, we glided to a majestic halt in Platform 1, with the little engine proudly staring out over the sea to Skye. A job well done, on time, the mails delivered, communities served, and a way of life maintained which at the time, looked like it would go on forever.